SOUTHERN COMFORT

Allison Vines-Rushing and Slade Rushing

Photography by Ed Anderson

SOUTHERN COMFORT

A NEW TAKE ON THE RECIPES
WE GREW UP WITH

TEN SPEED PRESS
Berkeley

CONTENTS

THIS BOOK IS DEDICATED TO IDA LOU VINES-RUSHING,
THE SWEETEST LITTLE DISH WE HAVE EVER CREATED.

OUR STORY

WE MET IN THE KITCHEN OF A RESTAURANT called
Gerard's Downtown in New Orleans. It was the fall of
2000, we were both cooks and we fell in love. Six months
later, we purchased two one-way tickets to New York
City on the City of New Orleans train and away we went.
We each landed jobs and rented a tiny one-room base-
ment apartment in Brooklyn complete with a patch of
dirt in the back. We planted a garden and felt like the
two luckiest people on Earth.

Working in New York was more mentally and physi-
cally exhausting than we had imagined, but our Southern
stubbornness prevented us from giving up. We also had
our little Brooklyn refuge, where on late nights after work
(Slade was at March and I was at Ducasse), wine revived
our tired bodies, and we created dishes and wrote menus
sprinkled with comforting memories from home. Funny
how soon those ideas would come in handy. After only a
few years in New York, we became head chefs of a tiny restaurant in the East Village called Jack's Luxury Oyster Bar.

Finding ourselves at Jack's was serendipitous to say
the least. At the time, Slade was *chef de cuisine* at a little

1

French restaurant in the Flatiron District called Fleur de Sel, and I had just left Ducasse to take a break from the stress and plan our wedding. I applied for a job as a barista at the recently opened Blue Goose Café, armed with a ridiculous résumé that included all of my restaurant experience from the last ten years—starting with Kenny Roger's Roasters in Coral Springs, Florida, and ending with Alain Ducasse. Jack Lamb, the owner of the Blue Goose, checked out my résumé and said he wanted to hire me as the chef of a new restaurant he was opening. I was a bit taken aback, but saying no was never my strong suit. I said yes, but told him I was getting married in August—to which he replied, "Then we will open the restaurant in September." I immediately called Slade to tell him I had gotten a job, but as a chef. He asked me if I had lost my mind.

On the opening night of Jack's Luxury Oyster Bar (which was also my twenty-eighth birthday), Slade took the night off from Fleur de Sel to cook by my side. A few months later, on Valentine's Day of 2004, he joined me as the co-chef at Jack's. There, our menus were riffs on classic New Orleans dishes, mingled with French-inspired soul food. Customers walked through the kitchen to get into the upstairs dining room, while we scrubbed our own pots and pans in a little sink after we served each table. Our tiny seven by seven-foot kitchen with a Sub-Zero fridge and four-burner stove was about as far away from a commercial restaurant kitchen as you could get. There was no walk-in cooler and no real prep space to speak of, so we packed the small fridge every day before service and emptied it out before the end of the night. The spiral staircase in the middle of the kitchen became our cooling

rack. It was a job no chef in their right mind would agree to take on, but lucky for us we did and we made it work. Pretty soon the customers walking through the unconventional kitchen were chefs like David Bouley, Jeremiah Towers, Alain Ducasse, Eric Ripert, François Payard, and many others. Lines formed outside to wait for tables. We realized that something special was going on.

But too quickly, it all got much bigger than us. The media attention was constant and hugely flattering—and, well, tricky. All of the positive press resulted in customers' increasing expectations, plus our egos grew, things became complicated with our boss, and the honeymoon was definitely over for our brand-new marriage. We decided to get the hell out of town. The article in the *New York Times* read "Two Rising Stars Opt Out of Manhattan." What a way to go.

We unpacked our bags in Abita Springs, right outside of New Orleans, three months before the most disastrous hurricane ever hit this area. Our family had bought us an amazing, dreamy property, which would become our first restaurant, Longbranch. We had the "we made it in New York, we can make it anywhere" attitude. And then all hell broke loose. A week before the restaurant was set to open, we packed up our truck to evacuate before Katrina hit. We took a couple of changes of clothes, beer, foie gras and sweetbreads that we didn't want to go bad, and two dogs that weren't ours. We headed to Tylertown, Mississippi, and didn't return home for over a week. Even in Mississippi we were not completely out of Katrina's path, and the power was not restored there until after we had headed back home. Luckily, Slade's sister Kim had a natural spring well in her backyard, so we rigged up a shower where we could also wash dishes and clothes. To keep ourselves busy, we raided all the freezers on our street and then cooked friends, family, and neighbors three meals a day on a gas grill.

Upon returning to Abita Springs, we hadn't a clue what would be waiting for us. We had given friends in town who did not evacuate the key to the restaurant in case the worse happened. They had cleaned out the walk-in cooler of food to sustain themselves and their neighbors for the week, so thankfully we didn't have to deal with rotten, moldy food. We found that most of the trees on the property had fallen, and the cottage we were living in was in very bad shape. The restaurant building, however, looked mostly unscathed. The energy company was there to turn back on the electricity, so we began cleaning up. Longbranch quietly opened one week later.

For dinner, we served the same food that garnered us attention at Jack's. Our Sunday brunches were an instant success, and we even had a two-piece jazz band come play. (They had lost their steady gig at Commander's Palace in New Orleans, which had not yet reopened after the storm.) We hoped what we were offering at Long-branch would give our recently scarred customers a momentary escape away from it all. But a fine dining restaurant with no history in the area and very high overhead eventually got the better of us. We closed the doors after a turbulent year-and-a-half-long run.

Before we closed Longbranch, a customer, Frank Zumbo, asked if we would be interested in opening a restaurant in a Marriott hotel in New Orleans. MiLa— named for our respective home states, Mississippi and Louisiana—was born in November of 2007 in the

Renaissance Pere Marquette. We are still serving our Southern-flecked cuisine, although the menu is considerably bigger than that first menu at Jack's (which had one entrée and one dessert). The dishes we created back then, such as Oysters Rockefeller "Deconstructed" and New Orleans–Style Barbecue Lobster, have traveled with us from Jack's to Longbranch, then to MiLa, and now to this book. For simplicity's sake, in the book we have broken down a lot of the dishes we serve at the restaurant into separate components. We've also sprinkled some favorite childhood recipes in between. We hope the food in this book represents who we are, where we are from, and the places we have been.

Five years after opening MiLa, life is sweet again. We have four beautiful bloodhounds, an old fishing boat with lots of character, a home where we can lay down some roots, and a brand new baby girl. The delicate balance of work and play has become a reality. And the food tastes better, too.

BREAKFAST AND BREADS

BREAKFAST AND BREADS

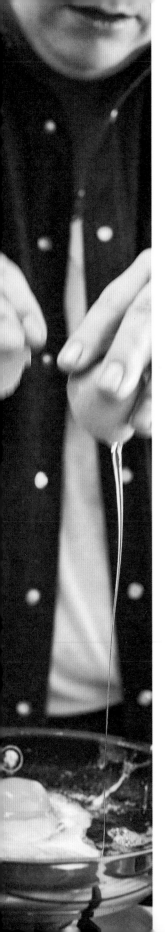

THE MEAL SLADE AND I most cherish is breakfast. In our business, lunch and dinner are working hours, making mornings our one-on-one time. It is a bonus that it is the mealtime that serves up our most favorite foods: eggs over easy for me, cheese grits for Slade, griddled ham, pecan waffles, biscuits with mayhaw jelly for both of us. Sure, here and there we have to settle for a bowl of cereal, but it just makes the warm breakfasts we get to linger over that much more special.

Breakfast is so special, in fact, that we incorporated our favorite meal into our wedding vows. We wrote our own the night before our wedding in our last-minute style, and I am a bit ashamed to admit that "I promise to make you breakfast every other Sunday" is the only one that I remember eight years later. Of course, love, honor, cherish, and all that good stuff must have been in there too, but those words did not elicit the robust belly laughs from our small audience that our breakfast vow did. It brightened our afternoon ceremony just like the morning sunshine.

NEW ORLEANS–STYLE GRITS AND GRILLADES

SERVES 4

Gerard's Downtown, a New Orleans restaurant that closed shortly after 9/11, was the most influential restaurant in our lives. Not only did we meet and fall in love while working there, the chef-owner Gerard Maras, who was really ahead of his time, was the kind of chef we both wanted to become. His simple, refined touch elevated Creole cuisine and his farm-to-table approach gave birth to the new guard of chefs in New Orleans.

When we opened Longbranch after Katrina in September of 2005, Gerard offered his help in getting our restaurant up and running. Cooks were impossible to find and when you did find them, their salary demands were storm-inflated. The two of us, Gerard, and one other cook, Trey Helmka, comprised our opening kitchen staff. This man, who taught us so much, was beside us on the line, and the comfort of his presence in the kitchen was priceless. How ironic that at Sunday brunches at Longbranch he was cooking our version of Grits and Grillades, a country pork stew we learned to cook from him. Here is a simplified version using pork tenderloin.

1 pork tenderloin (about 1^1/$_2$ pounds)

1^1/$_2$ cups all-purpose flour

1 teaspoon salt

1 teaspoon freshly ground black pepper

3 tablespoons canola oil

8 slices bacon, diced

1 red bell pepper, diced

1 green bell pepper, diced

1 onion, diced

1 tablespoon chopped garlic

1 tablespoon Creole spice (page 222)

1 teaspoon ground cumin

1 teaspoon paprika

2 bay leaves

4 cups chicken stock (page 220)

1 ripe tomato, chopped, cored, juices reserved

Creamy Grits (recipe follows)

4 green onions, white and green parts, thinly sliced
    (for garnish)

Cut the pork tenderloin into twelve 2-ounce cutlets. Place each cutlet between sheets of plastic wrap. Using a meat mallet, pound each medallion until it is a uniform thickness of about 1/8 inch.

In a baking dish large enough to hold a cutlet, mix 1 cup of the flour with 1/2 teaspoon of the salt and 1/2 teaspoon of the pepper until fully incorporated. Lightly dust each cutlet in the flour mixture on both sides; set aside on a plate until ready to cook.

For the cutlets, have a plate ready. For the bacon, line a plate with paper towels and have ready.

Heat a 12-inch cast-iron skillet over medium heat until slightly smoking. Add 1 tablespoon of the oil and sauté the cutlets in batches, four at a time. Cook them for 1 minute on each side, then transfer from the pan to the plate and repeat with the remaining oil and cutlets.

Once all of the pork is cooked, keep the skillet on medium heat and add the bacon to it. Cook the bacon until the fat is fully rendered out. With a slotted spoon, remove the bacon from the pan to the paper-lined plate and reserve it on the side, leaving the fat in the pan. Decrease the heat to low and whisk in the remaining 1/2 cup of flour until smooth and the consistency of wet sand. Cook, whisking constantly until the roux becomes light brown and nutty, about 10 minutes. Add the diced bell peppers, onion, and garlic and cook the vegetables in the roux until tender, about 3 minutes.

Carefully whisk in the remaining 1/2 teaspoon salt and 1/2 teaspoon pepper, Creole spice, cumin, paprika, and bay leaves. Once the spices are incorporated, whisk in the stock and chopped tomato with its juices until a smooth sauce is formed. Increase the heat to medium and bring the sauce to a low simmer. Decrease the heat to low and simmer for 10 minutes, skimming off any excess fat. Strain the sauce through a sieve and return it to the skillet. Place the pork cutlets in the sauce and warm them through.

Serve the pork in the sauce over the grits and garnish with the sliced green onions.

CREAMY GRITS

8 cups whole milk
2 cups quick grits
1 cup unsalted butter, cut into pieces
1/2 cup heavy cream
1 tablespoon salt
2 teaspoons freshly ground black pepper

Place the milk in a medium saucepan over medium heat until it scalds (when a skin forms on top, and it begins to bubble around the edges). Whisk the grits into the milk and decrease the heat to medium-low. Cook for 10 minutes, whisking occasionally to prevent clumps. Finish the grits by whisking in the butter, heavy cream, salt, and pepper. Cover with a lid, remove from the heat, and reserve until serving. It will stay hot for about 20 minutes, covered.

SMOKED REDFISH AND FARM EGG SALAD

SERVES 4

This is our version of *frisée aux lardons,* the classic French salad. Pairing feathery bitter lettuce and bacon with unctuous soft-boiled egg, it's a salad that easily serves as a main course. Our lagniappe of lightly smoked redfish makes this salad perfect for brunch. If you cannot find redfish, good substitutes are pompano or Spanish mackerel. You'll need a stovetop smoker for the redfish (see Sources, page 223).

12 ounces redfish fillets, boned and skinned

1 teaspoon red pepper flakes

1 tablespoon soy sauce

2 tablespoons honey

4 ounces applewood smoked bacon, finely diced

2 shallots, finely diced

2 cloves garlic, minced

2 tablespoons sherry vinegar

1/4 cup canola oil

1 tablespoon extra-virgin olive oil

1/2 teaspoon fine sea salt

1/2 teaspoon freshly ground black pepper

6 heads frisée (curly endive)

1/4 cup distilled white vinegar

4 large farm eggs

4 ounces fresh chives, chopped

Put the redfish fillets in a rimmed dish.

To make the marinade, in a small bowl, whisk together the red pepper flakes, soy sauce, and 1 tablespoon of the honey and pour over the fish. Let the fish marinate for 1 hour.

To make the vinaigrette, add the bacon to a sauté pan and cook over low heat, stirring occasionally, until the fat is rendered and the bacon is crispy, about 10 minutes. Pour off half the fat and add the shallots and garlic. Cook until the shallots and garlic are translucent, stirring constantly with a wooden spoon to prevent burning. Add the sherry vinegar and the remaining 1 tablespoon honey then

cook until reduced by half. Pour into a bowl and let cool. Whisk in the canola and olive oils, the 1/2 teaspoon salt, and 1/2 teaspoon pepper; reserve.

To prepare the frisée, fill a large bowl with ice water. Grab a pair of sharp scissors and hold the frisée heads with one hand. Cut off all the bitter green pieces and discard them. Next, cut the remaining frisée into little clusters into the ice water. Wash well and dry thoroughly in a salad spinner.

To smoke the redfish, place 1 cup hickory chips in the rear of the bottom of a stovetop smoker. Remove the fish from the marinade and arrange the fillets on the rack of the smoker, positioning them in the front of the smoker away from the wood chips. Set the stovetop smoker on your cooktop so the rear is on top of a back burner, and the front of the smoker sits on a front burner. Set only the rear burner to high and let the smoker sit over high heat until a steady smoke drifts out of the smoker. Decrease the heat to low and continue to smoke for 5 minutes.

Remove the fillets from the smoker. Quickly break them into large flakes with your hands and reserve on a plate.

To poach the eggs, add 12 cups of water and the distilled vinegar to a large saucepan

CONTINUED

and bring to a boil over high heat, then reduce to medium-low heat for a slow simmer.

Meanwhile, to finish the salad, put the frisée, redfish, and vinaigrette in a large bowl and season with salt and pepper. Mix the salad well and divide it among four plates.

Stir the simmering vinegar water, then crack the eggs into it, one by one. Cook the eggs for 2 minutes and then, with a slotted spoon, remove them one at a time, placing one egg on each salad. Garnish with fresh chives.

SPINACH AND CRAWFISH OMELET WITH CHORON SAUCE

SERVES 4

Choron is a hollandaise sauce with the essence of tomato and tarragon. Hollandaise has a special place our relationship. On our first Valentine's Day, we were working together at Gerard's Downtown. Slade was on his station furiously—and secretively—creating. He then brought over a breakfast made just for me. It was two poached eggs with heart-shaped toasts, bacon fashioned into Cupid's arrows, and "I Love You" written in hollandaise. I was a goner.

CHORON SAUCE

1/2 cup canned plum tomatoes in juice (about
    2 tomatoes), pureed in a blender

Sprig of tarragon

4 large egg yolks

Juice of 1 lemon

2 cups unsalted butter, each stick cut into quarters

1 tablespoon water

1/2 teaspoon white wine vinegar

2 dashes hot sauce

1/4 teaspoon fine sea salt

SPINACH-CRAWFISH OMELETS

8 large eggs

6 tablespoons unsalted butter

8 ounces baby spinach (about 4 cups)

4 ounces crawfish tails, deveined

Salt and freshly ground black pepper

To make the sauce, in a small saucepan over medium heat, cook the tomato puree with the tarragon sprig until there is no more liquid, and the puree is reduced to about 1 tablespoon. Discard the tarragon sprig. Set the tomato puree aside.

Place the butter in a small microwave-safe bowl and microwave on high until the butter is completely melted, about 2 1/2 minutes. Remove the butter from the microwave and let sit for a few minutes; skim off any foam that has formed on the top and discard. Pour the clear yellow butter into another dish, avoiding any of the milk solids in the bottom. This is clarified butter to use for the sauce.

In a small saucepan, combine the egg yolks and lemon juice and cook over low heat, whisking the mixture briskly until it starts to thicken. You may need to pull the pan on and off the heat to control the temperature so you don't scramble the egg yolks. Once the eggs are thickened, use a ladle to slowly drizzle half the clarified butter into the eggs while continuing to whisk.

Thin the sauce out a bit with the 1 tablespoon water to prevent the sauce from getting too tight and breaking. Continue adding the remaining butter and whisking. You should end up with a thick and silky emulsified sauce.

To finish the sauce, add the vinegar, hot sauce, salt, and reserved tomato puree and mix well with a whisk. Keep the sauce warm beside the stove or on a shelf above the stove (but not on direct heat) while you make the omelets.

To make the omelets, line a plate with paper towels and set aside. In a small bowl,

CONTINUED

whisk the eggs vigorously until they are a thin liquid.

Heat a large sauté pan over medium-high heat. Add 2 tablespoons of the butter to the pan and let it brown. Add the spinach, cooking just until wilted, then add the crawfish tails and cook until the mixture is warm. Season the mixture well with salt and pepper. Gently mix together the spinach and crawfish and remove to the prepared plate; reserve, keeping them warm until omelets are cooked.

Heat a nonstick skillet over medium heat. Melt 1 tablespoon of the butter. Add one-quarter of the whisked eggs to the pan and season with salt and pepper. With a rubber spatula, stir the eggs a bit until they start to set, then swirl the pan until the eggs coat the bottom in an even layer. Let the omelet cook a little to set up; once there is just a hint of wetness on the top, add one-quarter of the spinach and crawfish mixture to the center of the omelet. Using a rubber spatula, fold one side of the omelet over the filling. Then working over a plate, fold the omelet over once more, sliding onto a plate.

Repeat this process to make three more omelets, adding a tablespoon of butter for each.

Top each omelet with sauce and serve.

VANILLA FRENCH TOAST WITH BRANDY WHIPPED CREAM

SERVES 4

The key to this French toast is twofold: thick-cut bread and a lengthy soak in a decadent cream and egg base. Slowly browning the soaked bread in butter results in a crispy exterior and a delicate creamy interior. The fragrance of orange zest and vanilla perfectly mingles with a garnish of brandy-scented cream.

8 (1-inch-thick) slices brioche (page 31)

1/4 cup plus 2 tablespoons granulated sugar

4 large egg yolks

1 vanilla bean, split, seeds scraped, and pod discarded

4 cups heavy cream

Zest from 1 medium orange, grated

1 teaspoon orange juice

3 tablespoons brandy

2 tablespoons confectioners' sugar

1/2 cup unsalted butter, diced

To soak the bread, place the slices in a baking dish large enough to hold them in a single layer. In a large mixing bowl, whisk together the granulated sugar, egg yolks, and vanilla seeds until the mixture is creamy and light yellow. Slowly whisk in 2 cups of the heavy cream, then whisk in the orange zest, orange juice, and 2 tablespoons of the brandy. Pour the mixture over the bread slices, making sure to cover the slices completely. Soak the bread thoroughly, turning once, for a total of 10 minutes.

While the bread is soaking, with a stand mixer fitted with the whisk attachment,

whip the remaining 2 cups of heavy cream with the remaining 1 tablespoon of brandy and 1 tablespoon of the confectioners' sugar until it reaches stiff peaks. Reserve the whipped cream in the refrigerator (it will keep covered for up to 1 hour) until the French toast is ready to serve.

To cook the French toast, line a large platter with paper towels and have ready.

Heat a large sauté pan over medium-low heat and add half of the butter to the pan. Once the butter begins to foam, add half of the soaked bread to the pan and let them slowly brown. With a spatula, lift an edge of one slice to see if a nice brown crust has formed. If it has, flip the slices and cook until golden brown and crispy. Remove them from the pan to the prepared platter. Add the remaining butter and bread to the pan and repeat the process. If your pan isn't large enough to fit four slices at a time, you may have to do this in more than two batches.

To serve, place the toasts on a large platter and dust with the remaining 1 tablespoon of confectioners' sugar. Serve with the brandied whipped cream on the side.

SWEET POTATO PANCAKES (INSPIRED BY BRUCE'S)

Makes twelve 6-inch pancakes; serves 4

Our local supermarket, Rouses, takes pride in showcasing local produce and products. Cruising the aisles one day, we found a sweet potato pancake mix by Bruce's, made in New Iberia, Louisiana, which became one of our breakfast addictions. We have even given it out as Christmas gifts. After a while we began to feel a bit ashamed about not making pancakes from scratch, and we also missed the soufflé-like fluffiness you can only get from a freshly made batter. So we created this version. Make them on a winter morning, and serve covered in sweet syrup alongside salty smoky bacon.

1 large sweet potato
2 cups all-purpose flour
2 tablespoons sugar
2 teaspoons baking powder
1 teaspoon baking soda
1 teaspoon salt
1 teaspoon ground cinnamon
1/2 teaspoon freshly grated nutmeg
2 large eggs
1/2 cup whole milk
1 cup buttermilk
Unsalted butter, for the griddle
Maple syrup, for serving

Prick the sweet potato with a fork five times and microwave on high for 15 minutes. Holding the potato with a kitchen towel, halve it, scoop out the soft flesh, and transfer the pulp to a bowl. Mash with a fork or potato masher.

Preheat a griddle over medium-high heat.

In a large bowl, combine the flour, sugar, baking powder, baking soda, salt, cinnamon, and nutmeg and whisk until well incorporated. In a separate bowl, combine the eggs, milk, buttermilk, and mashed sweet potato and whisk them until well incorporated.

Make a well in the center of the dry ingredients, and pour the wet ingredients into the center of the well. Using a whisk and working from the inside to the out, whisk the wet ingredients into the dry ingredients, making a smooth pancake batter.

Melt the butter on the hot griddle. Using a 1/4-cup measuring cup, pour 1/4 cup of the batter onto the griddle for each pancake and smooth each into a circle with the back of a spoon. Once the pancakes begin to bubble, flip them over and cook for another minute. Tranfer the cooked pancakes to a plate and keep warm in a low oven. Repeat until all of the batter is used.

Serve immediately, smothered with syrup.

BANANA-RUM CRÊPES WITH BROWN SUGAR WHIPPED CREAM

SERVES 6

One of Slade's mentors, chef Cyril Renaud, taught him how to make a classic Normandy crêpe: thick with apples and with a crispy caramel coating. He served them topped with Devonshire cream. This particular crêpe is thick, more in the style of a pancake, and cooked in the pan with sugar and butter until golden brown with a crispy caramel crust. We give it a New Orleans spin with bananas, rum, and brown sugar à la bananas Foster.

3 large eggs

1 1/4 cups whole milk

1 cup all-purpose flour

1/4 teaspoon ground cinnamon

1/4 cup unsalted butter, melted

2 teaspoons dark rum

3 firm, ripe bananas

2 tablespoons unsalted butter, cold, cut into
  6 even-size dice

2 cups heavy cream

3/4 cup plus 2 tablespoons packed light brown sugar

Confectioners' sugar, for dusting

To make the crêpe batter, in a bowl, whisk together the eggs and milk until fully incorporated. In a separate bowl, whisk together the flour and the cinnamon. Next, slowly whisk the wet ingredients into the dry ingredients, moving from the inside to outside for a smooth batter. Strain the batter through a fine sieve into a bowl and then whisk in the melted butter and rum. Chill the batter, covered, in the refrigerator for at least 1 hour, and up to 24 hours.

To prepare the bananas, peel them, trim off the stem ends, and halve the fruit lengthwise. Slice each banana half crosswise into three pieces (you'll have eighteen pieces total); set aside.

Preheat the broiler.

While the broiler is heating, in a stand mixer fitted with the whisk attachment, whip the cream on medium-high speed until it reaches soft peaks. Add 2 tablespoons of the brown sugar and whip until it is thoroughly incorporated. Set aside.

Place an 8-inch nonstick ovenproof skillet over medium heat. Once the pan is warm, add one piece of the cold butter and three banana slices. Sauté the bananas until they are lightly golden on one side, then ladle 1/2 cup of crêpe batter into the pan. Using a rubber spatula, lightly push in the edges of the batter and swirl the pan as though you were making an omelet. Once the crêpe has formed in the pan, flip it over, spread 2 tablespoons of the remaining brown sugar evenly on top of the crêpe, and place the crêpe underneath the broiler. Once all the sugar has been caramelized and is a dark shiny amber color, carefully remove the crêpe from the pan and turn out onto a plate. Repeat the process for the rest of the crêpe batter and bananas.

Serve the crêpes dusted with confectioners' sugar and topped with whipped cream.

GREEN ONION AND GOAT CHEESE QUICHE

SERVES 8 TO 10

The combination of eggs and green onions make some people go to extreme measures. I remember one rainy, cold November morning when I was a boy, as my dad was preparing scrambled eggs for breakfast, he realized there were no more green onions in the fridge. Being a quick thinker, he suggested that I go steal a bunch from our neighbor's garden. As Dad melted the butter in the pan, I ran through the woods and stealthily approached the barbed wire fence surrounding Mr. Prescott's garden. Easing through the fence, I grabbed the onions and pulled them from the soft ground. As I stood there shaking the dirt from the roots, I heard Mr. Prescott yelling, followed by the sound of a shotgun firing into the air. I ran like hell home, managing to make it with a few onions unscathed. In this recipe, the green onions really are a requirement, but stealing them might not be the best idea.

Dough

1¹/4 cups all-purpose flour

1 teaspoon salt

1/2 teaspoon coarsely ground black pepper

1 cup unsalted butter, cold, cut into 1/4-inch dice

1/4 cup ice water

Filling

4 large egg yolks

1 large whole egg

2 cups heavy cream

1/2 teaspoon fine sea salt

1 bunch (about 8) green onions, white and
    green parts, thinly sliced

4 ounces goat cheese

Preheat the oven to 350°F.

To make the dough, in the bowl of a food processor fitted with the metal blade, combine the flour, salt, and black pepper and pulse once to mix the ingredients. Add the diced butter and pulse until the butter is the size of peas. Then, while pulsing, add the ice water in a slow drizzle. Turn the dough out onto a lightly floured work surface. Pull it together into a ball and press firmly. Shape into a flat disk. Wrap it in plastic wrap and chill the dough for at least 30 minutes.

Meanwhile, prepare the filling. In a bowl, combine the egg yolks and whole egg and whisk together well. Add the cream and the salt and whisk until everything is fully incorporated. Chill thoroughly.

To finish the crust, using a rolling pin, roll out the pie dough on a lightly floured work surface into 14-inch round that is 1/8 inch thick. Transfer the pie crust to a 10-inch diameter pie dish and trim and crimp the edges. Pierce the crust with the fork all over the bottom. Line the bottom of the crust with parchment paper and cover the paper with dried beans or raw rice to weight down the crust. Bake for 15 minutes.

Remove the crust from the oven and carefully lift off and discard the parchment paper and pie weights. Fill the crust with the filling and green onions, and dot the surface evenly with the goat cheese.

Bake the quiche until lightly browned on top and firm to the touch, 20 to 25 minutes. Let the quiche cool for at least 30 minutes before cutting into wedges and serving.

SHALLOT CORNBREAD

MAKES ABOUT 30 THREE-INCH PIECES

This recipe was a complete accident. One night at Jack's, I was making cornbread and when I pulled it from the oven, it was totally flat. Slade was a bit upset with me for forgetting the baking powder in the recipe until he tasted it. It was cornbread, but dense, flavorful, and not crumbly, making it a great vehicle for spreads and toppings, such as lima bean dip (page 59) or Smoked Fish Spread (page 52). A complete screw-up on my part became a bread we have served in our restaurants ever since. Freeze the leftovers tightly wrapped in plastic wrap (they'll keep for up to 6 months) to use for cornbread croutons later.

2 cups all-purpose flour

2 cups cornmeal

2 teaspoons salt

4 large eggs

2 cups whole milk

1 cup unsalted butter, melted and cooled to
　　room temperature

3 shallots, finely diced

Preheat the oven to 400°F. Line an 11 by 17-inch baking sheet with parchment paper and coat with a nice layer of olive oil.

In a large bowl, whisk together the flour, cornmeal, and salt. In a separate bowl, whisk together the eggs and milk. Make a well in the center of the dry ingredients and slowly pour the wet ingredients into the center of the well. Whisk the two together, working from the inside out, until they are completely combined. Whisk the melted butter into the cornbread mixture, and then fold in the diced shallots with a rubber spatula. Spread the cornbread mixture evenly onto the baking sheet and bake until the edges are brown and the center is firm, 15 to 18 minutes.

To serve, let the bread cool slightly and turn the pan upside down to remove the cornbread. Using a serrated knife, cut the bread into 3-inch squares and serve hot.

CRÈME FRAÎCHE BISCUITS

MAKES ABOUT 22 BISCUITS

Southerners take pride in a good biscuit in the same way the French do with puff pastry. Biscuit dough is equally versatile—make it into dumplings, roll and use as a topping, fry it like doughnuts—but infinitely easier to make than its French counterpart. There are just a couple of things you must do to achieve success with biscuit dough: use very cold butter and don't overwork the dough. This biscuit is made with crème fraîche, which adds a bit of acidity, making it a perfect partner for homemade jam. If you don't have crème fraîche, just substitute sour cream.

4 cups all-purpose flour, plus more for dusting

2 tablespoons baking powder

2 teaspoons fine sea salt

1 teaspoon sugar

1 cup unsalted butter, cold, cut into tablespoons

1 1/4 cups heavy cream, plus more for brushing

1/2 cup crème fraîche (page 221)

1 large egg

Melted unsalted butter for brushing (optional)

Preheat the oven to 400°F.

In a large bowl, whisk together the flour, baking powder, salt, and sugar. Working quickly with your fingers, cut the butter into the flour until the butter is the size of peas. In a small bowl, whisk together the cream, crème fraîche, and egg to combine. Make a well in the center of the flour-butter mixture and slowly pour the wet ingredients into the center of the well. Stir the ingredients together with a fork until the dough is evenly moistened, then turn the dough out onto a lightly floured work surface.

Knead the biscuit dough gently, no more than 10 kneads, until it holds together, being careful not to overwork the dough.

With a rolling pin, roll the dough out to a thickness of 1 inch. Cut out biscuits with a 2-inch round biscuit cutter and place on non-stick baking sheets about 1 1/2 inches apart. Gently press the scraps together to stamp out more biscuits or wrap them tightly and freeze for later use as a topping for chicken pot pie.

Refrigerate the tray of biscuits until they are chilled and firm, about 30 minutes. Brush the tops with a touch of heavy cream or melted butter and bake until they are golden on top, about 18 minutes.

Serve hot with butter and jam.

BUTTERMILK BRIOCHE

This butter-rich bread is undeniably best served warm when it can melt in your mouth. For the best result, be sure to do two things: First, work the dough well in the mixer as it needs the kneading for structure. Second, be sure to bake it until the crust is dark brown—don't pull it out of the oven too soon, otherwise it will deflate. Serve it at brunch with your favorite preserves or use it to make a most decadent French toast (page 24).

1 cup warm buttermilk (100°F to 110°F)

1 package (2$1/4$ teaspoons) instant dry yeast

2 cups all-purpose flour

2$1/3$ cups cake flour

$1/3$ cup sugar

2$1/2$ teaspoons salt

4 large eggs

1 cup plus 2 tablespoons unsalted butter, cut into
   $1/2$-inch dice, at room temperature

Preheat the oven to 350°F.

Put the warm buttermilk in the bowl of a stand mixer and stir in the yeast with a wooden spoon until dissolved. Stir 1 cup of the all-purpose flour into the buttermilk mixture, also with the wooden spoon. Cover the bowl with plastic wrap and place in a warm area of the kitchen until doubled in size, about 1 hour.

Return the bowl to the stand mixer fitted with the paddle attachment. Add the remaining 1 cup all-purpose flour, cake flour, sugar, and salt and mix on low speed until com-

bined. Add the eggs, one at a time, mixing well between each addition, until a batter-like dough is formed. Replace the paddle with the dough hook attachment. Mix the dough on low speed for 10 minutes. Add the butter in three increments, letting the dough absorb all of the butter each time, then mix on low speed for an additional 20 minutes, making sure that all the butter is incorporated into the dough.

Spray a 10 by 6 by 3-inch nonstick loaf pan with nonstick cooking spray.

Place the dough on a lightly floured surface. Divide it into five equal portions and roll each into a ball. Place the dough balls side by side in the prepared loaf pan. Proof the bread by placing it in a warm area, covered with plastic wrap, until it has doubled in size, about 30 minutes.

Bake until the crust is a dark mahogany brown, about 25 minutes. Let it cool for 30 minutes, then remove the bread from the pan and slice.

SWEET POTATO ROLLS

MAKES 12 ROLLS

We have lots of fans of the soft sweet potato rolls we serve at the restaurant, but probably the biggest fan is Slade's young cousin Burke. He came to the restaurant for dinner and was quite enamored of the rolls. So much so that he ate a baker's dozen slathered with salted butter and honey, then asked for a few more to take home.

1¹/2 pounds sweet potatoes (about 3 medium)

¹/2 cup warm whole milk (100°F to 110°F)

1 package (2¹/4 teaspoons) instant dry yeast

2¹/2 cups all-purpose flour, plus additional flour for rolling

¹/2 cup packed light brown sugar

¹/4 cup extra-virgin olive oil

¹/2 cup unsalted butter, melted

1¹/2 teaspoons salt

Salted butter, for serving

Prick each sweet potato with a fork five times and microwave them together on high for 15 minutes. Holding a hot potato with a kitchen towel set in the palm of your hand, halve each potato, scoop out the soft flesh, and transfer the pulp to the bowl of a food processor fitted with the metal blade. Discard the potato skins. Puree the pulp until smooth. Let the puree cool and set aside until needed.

Preheat the oven to 325°F. Spray a baking sheet with nonstick cooking spray.

Pour the warm milk into a bowl; whisk in the yeast until dissolved. Using a wooden spoon, stir ¹/2 cup of the flour into the milk mixture until it is absorbed. Cover the bowl with plastic wrap and place in a warm area of the kitchen until it has doubled in size, about 1 hour. Combine the sweet potato puree, brown sugar, and olive oil in the bowl of a stand mixer fitted with the paddle attachment and mix until smooth. Add the melted butter, the remaining 2 cups flour, and the salt, along with yeast mixture and mix on low speed until the dough starts pulling from the sides of the bowl, about 10 minutes more. Place the dough on a lightly floured surface and divide into twelve equal portions.

Dust your work surface lightly with flour again if necessary and form the dough into balls. Place them 1 inch apart on the prepared baking sheet. Cover with plastic wrap and let the rolls rise until they have doubled in size, about 45 minutes. Remove the plastic wrap and bake for about 12 minutes.

Serve warm with salted butter.

PECAN-CHESTNUT BREAD

MAKES 1 LOAF

When Slade was the pastry chef at Rubicon in San Francisco, he learned a lot about wine from sommelier Larry Stone. Larry was passionate about more than wine, though. He was just as passionate about cheese. He would smuggle cheeses in his suitcase back from France and bring them to the restaurant for everyone to try. He also shared with Slade the recipe for his favorite bread to serve with those cheeses—a dense, hearty loaf packed with nuts.

1 1/2 cups warm whole milk (100°F to 110°F)

1 package (2 1/4 teaspoons) instant dry yeast

2 1/4 cups all-purpose flour

2 1/2 cups whole wheat flour

3/4 cup chestnuts, finely chopped

3/4 cup pecans, finely chopped

3 tablespoons honey

2 tablespoons molasses

1 tablespoon salt

1 teaspoon extra-virgin olive oil

Preheat the oven to 350°F.

Pour the warm water into the bowl of a stand mixer and, using a wooden spoon, stir in the yeast until it has dissolved. Next add 1 cup of the all-purpose flour and give a gentle stir, also by hand, to mix the flour into the liquid. Cover the bowl with plastic wrap and place in a warm area of the kitchen until doubled in size, about 1 hour.

Line a baking sheet with parchment paper or have a nonstick baking sheet ready.

Return the bowl to the stand mixer fitted with the hook attachment. Add the remaining 1 1/4 cups all-purpose flour, whole wheat flour, chestnuts, pecans, honey, molasses, salt, and olive oil. Mix on low speed for 20 minutes to form the dough.

Transfer the dough to a lightly floured surface. Using the palm of your hands, pat the dough into a large, flat oval about 1 inch thick. With both hands, tightly roll the dough into a cylinder and place on the prepared baking sheet, seam side down. Bake until the bread is dark brown and crusty, about 45 minutes. Let it cool for 30 minutes before slicing and serving.

COCKTAIL FARE

COCKTAIL FARE

INSPIRED COCKTAIL FOOD should be just as fun and juicy as the cocktail party itself. Bite-size, easy-to-eat food is imperative, because something hanging from the side of your mouth or staining the front of your shirt is a real conversation killer. Some guests may try to avoid embarrassment by using the "eat first, mingle later" approach, but too much lingering alone around the food runs the risk of putting out a piggy, antisocial vibe. You can make your cocktail party one that everyone enjoys by anticipating the needs of your hungry-to-eat, but also hungry-to-be-appropriate guests. Split up your food around the room to encourage movement and serve some of our tried-and-true crowd pleasers.

HUSH PUPPIES WITH CAVIAR

MAKES 24 PIECES

After an intense Saturday night service at Jack's Luxury Oyster Bar in New York, we would treat ourselves to a swanky meal at Blue Ribbon, the popular late-night hangout in SoHo. The maitre'd, Jason, was from Alabama and he always hooked us up with a table—no matter how many people were waiting. We dined on caviar and oysters and drank Sancerre. The only thing that could have made it better would have been a basket of hot hush puppies for cradling the salty caviar. For caviar, we use local choupique, but paddlefish is nice as well.

Canola or other neutral vegetable oil, for deep frying

2 cups cornmeal, finely ground in a blender

1 cup all-purpose flour

1 tablespoon baking powder

2 tablespoons sugar

1 teaspoon salt

1/2 teaspoon finely ground black pepper

1 1/2 cups buttermilk

2 large eggs

2 shallots, minced

2 tablespoon unsalted butter, melted

1/4 cup crème fraîche (page 221)

1/4 cup chopped fresh chives

4 ounces caviar

Fill a heavy, deep saucepan with at least 6 inches of oil. Heat the oil over medium-high heat until it registers 340°F on a deep-fry thermometer.

Meanwhile, in a large bowl, whisk together the cornmeal, flour, baking powder, sugar, salt, and pepper. In a separate small bowl, whisk together the buttermilk and eggs. Make a well in the center of the dry ingredients and pour in the wet ingredients. Mix with a whisk moving from the inside out until you have a smooth batter.

Add the shallots to the batter and fold them in completely. Then add the melted butter and mix until the batter is nice and smooth.

Line a plate with paper towels and have nearby. Using a 1-ounce ice cream scoop or just a large spoon, scoop the batter and drop into the hot oil, no more than five at a time. Fry until nice and golden brown, about 3 minutes, then remove and drain on the prepared plate.

To serve, halve each hush puppy and trim the bottoms flat so they stand up on a plate. Top each hush puppy half with caviar and crème fraîche and finish with chopped chives.

BLACK-EYED PEA EMPANADAS

MAKES ABOUT 30 SMALL EMPANADAS

When I attended high school in Coral Springs, Florida, I made a lifelong friend in Myra, whose Colombian mother, Lucy, referred to me as her "little rascal." I loved the warmth of their home, always full of aunts and cousins loudly chattering in Spanish while watching their soap operas (*novelas*). In the same house on a recent visit, Slade met the family over their homemade empanadas. This is a version we created—with a Southern touch of black-eyed peas and a green tomato–vinegar sauce.

2 cups all-purpose flour

1 tablespoon baking powder

2 teaspoons salt

1 cup unsalted butter, cold, cut into small dice

3 large egg yolks

2 tablespoons water

1 teaspoon white wine vinegar

1 tablespoon extra-virgin olive oil

2 shallots, diced

4 cloves garlic, thinly sliced

5 green onions, white and green parts, thinly sliced

2 1/4 teaspoons ground cumin

1/4 teaspoon Aleppo pepper, ground (see Sources, page 223)

1 1/2 cups cooked black-eyed peas

1 hard-boiled egg, peeled and chopped

2 large whole eggs, lightly beaten, for egg wash

Green Tomato–Vinegar Sauce, for accompaniment (recipe follows)

Preheat the oven to 350°F.

To make the dough, in a bowl, combine the flour, baking powder, and 1 teaspoon of the salt and whisk thoroughly. Add the diced butter to the flour mixture and working quickly, using your fingertips, combine them until the butter is in small, pea-size pieces. In a separate bowl, whisk together the egg yolks, water, and vinegar.

Make a well in the middle of the flour-butter mixture, then pour the wet ingredients into the well. Using your fingertips, stir the wet ingredients into the dry ingredients, until the mixture begins to clump together. Place the dough on a floured surface and knead until the dough becomes completely yellow and smooth, about 1 minute. Wrap the dough in plastic wrap and chill for 1 hour.

To make the filling, heat a large sauté pan over medium heat. Add the oil, shallots, and garlic and cook until the shallots begin to soften, about 3 minutes. Add the green onions, cumin, remaining 1 teaspoon of salt, and Aleppo pepper and cook until the spices are fragrant and the green onions soften, about 1 minute. Remove the pan from the heat and place the mixture in a bowl along with the black-eyed peas and chopped egg. Mix well.

To make the empanadas, place the chilled dough on a lightly floured work surface. Using a rolling pin, roll out the dough evenly until it is about 1/8 inch thick. With a 3-inch round biscuit cutter, cut the dough into circles. Place 1 heaping teaspoon of filling in the center of each circle. Brush the edges with the egg wash and fold in half over the filling, forming a half-moon shape. Press the edges together and seal with the tines of a fork. Arrange the empanadas on a nonstick baking sheet, spaced evenly apart. Bake until golden brown, about 15 minutes.

Serve warm with Green Tomato–Vinegar Sauce.

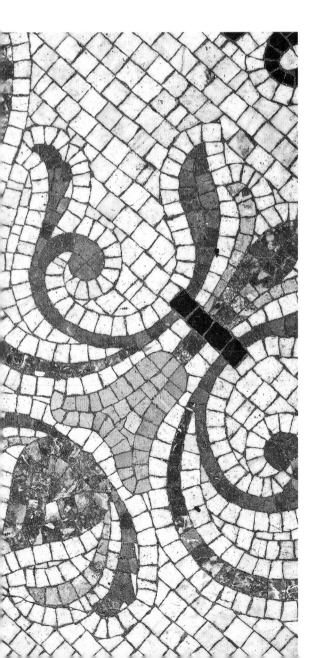

GREEN TOMATO–VINEGAR SAUCE

1 green tomato, cut into 4 wedges

1 jalepeño chile

1 cup tightly packed fresh cilantro leaves

4 cloves garlic, thinly sliced

3 green onions, white and green parts, thinly sliced

1 teaspoon fine sea salt

1 teaspoon Aleppo pepper, ground (see Sources, page 223)

1/2 teaspoon freshly ground black pepper

1/4 cup champagne vinegar

1/4 cup light olive oil

1 teaspoon agave nectar

Using the tip of your knife, remove the seeds from each tomato wedge and discard them. Cut the wedges into small dice and put the dice in a small bowl. Halve the jalapeño chile, remove the seeds from one of the halves, but leave them in the other for a bit of heat. Dice the chile and add to the tomatoes in the bowl. Add the cilantro, garlic, green onions, salt, Aleppo pepper, black pepper, vinegar, oil, and agave nectar, and mix until well combined.

ROASTED DUCK SPRING ROLLS WITH SATSUMA MUSTARD

MAKES 20 SPRING ROLLS

This duck and cabbage filling is so good, it is hard not to eat it straight up! It must be the chopped bits of crispy duck skin that makes it so addictive. We love to turn it into the filling for tiny little spring rolls, perfect for holiday parties. For spring roll wrappers, we like Spring Home brand (labeled "spring roll pastry"), stocked in the refrigerator or freezer section of supermarkets. There are twenty-five 8-inch-square wrappers in a package. Alternately, if you are a fan of the Chinese dish mu shu like we are, make a quick version with this filling, flour tortillas, and a jar of plum sauce.

2 duck legs

1 teaspoon Creole spice (page 222)

3 shallots, julienned

1 teaspoon chopped garlic

1 large carrot, julienned

1 head savoy cabbage, cored and julienned

1 tablespoon light brown sugar

1/2 teaspoon salt

1/2 cup chopped, toasted pecans

20 (8-inch-square) spring roll wrappers
    (see headnote)

1 large egg

Canola or other neutral vegetable oil, for frying

Satsuma Mustard, for accompaniment
    (recipe follows)

To make the filling, preheat the oven to 400°F.

Season the duck legs all over with Creole spice. Place in an ovenproof sauté pan and roast in the oven until the skin is brown and crispy, 30 to 45 minutes. Remove the pan from the oven. To test if the duck legs are done, wiggle the leg bone. It should easily twist away from the thigh bone if it is ready. Transfer the duck legs to a plate to cool and discard all but 2 tablespoons of the rendered duck fat in the pan.

Place the sauté pan on a burner over medium heat. Add the shallots, garlic, and carrots to the pan and cook for 2 minutes to soften, stirring occasionally with a wooden spoon and scraping the bottom of the pan. Once the vegetables are soft, add the cabbage, brown sugar, salt, and pecans and cook until the cabbage has softened, about 3 more minutes. Remove the pan from the heat and let the filling cool.

While the filling is cooling, remove the bones from the duck legs and finely chop the duck skin and the duck meat. Fold the meat into the cooled filling.

Fill a heavy, deep saucepan with at least 6 inches of oil. Heat the oil over medium-high heat until it registers 340°F on a deep-fry thermometer.

To assemble the spring rolls, arrange 20 spring roll wrappers on a work surface; cover with slightly damp paper towels to keep them moist. In a small bowl, vigorously whisk the egg.

For each spring roll, turn the wrapper so it faces you in a diamond shape. Dip two fingers in the beaten egg and brush it all around the edge of the wrapper. Place 2 tablespoons of filling in the center of the wrapper and fold the right and left sides of the wrapper, overlapping, over the filling. Pull the bottom corner up and over the filling and using your fingers, lay it over the filling into a tight log. Roll up the spring roll tightly, like a cigar. Repeat with the rest of the wrappers and filling.

Fry the spring rolls, a few at a time, until they are crispy and brown, about 1 minute.

Serve right away with Satsuma Mustard.

SATSUMA MUSTARD

10 satsumas (you can substitute clementines or
    mandarins)
1/4 cup Dijon mustard
2 tablespoons Creole mustard (see Sources, page 223)
    or any country-style whole-grain mustard
2 tablespoons champagne vinegar
1 tablespoon honey

With a knife, remove the peel from the satsumas and cut the satsumas into segments (supremes).

Place the segments into a saucepan and cook over medium heat until it is reduced by two-thirds. Let the reduction cool, then add the Dijon and Creole mustards, vinegar, and honey and whisk together until fully incorporated.

This will keep in the refrigerator for up to a week.

COCONUT SHRIMP BEIGNETS WITH PEPPER JELLY SAUCE

MAKES 20 TO 25 BEIGNETS

While traditional beignets are on the must-have list of every New Orleans tourist, we personally think flavor-wise they can be a bit one note. This version, however, is sweet and savory with a spicy dipping sauce. The addition of coconut and shrimp honor the Caribbean persuasions of New Orleans cuisine.

Canola oil or other neutral vegetable oil, for deep frying

1 cup pepper jelly (we use Tabasco brand; see Sources, page 223)

2 tablespoons Creole mustard (see Sources, page 223) or any country-style whole-grain mustard

2 tablespoons champagne vinegar (apple cider vinegar is a good substitute)

2 cups all-purpose flour

1 cup shredded sweetened coconut

1 tablespoon baking powder

1 teaspoon salt

1/2 teaspoon cayenne pepper

1/4 cup very thinly sliced green onions, white and green parts

1 (12-ounce) bottle of amber beer (we use Abita amber, but any amber will do)

Water (optional)

1 pound small shrimp, peeled and deveined

Fill a heavy, deep saucepan with at least 6 inches of oil. Heat the oil over medium-high heat until it registers 340°F on a deep-fry thermometer.

To make the sauce, combine the jelly, mustard, and vinegar; whisk until smooth and chill until needed (this can be made 1 day in advance).

To make the batter, in a large bowl, combine the flour, coconut, baking powder, salt, cayenne pepper, and green onions. Whisk the ingredients together thoroughly and make a well in the center.

Slowly pour the beer into the well, whisking from the inside to the outside until the mixture has the consistency of pancake batter. If it's not, thin it with a touch of water.

Line a plate with paper towels and have ready. Fold the shrimp into the batter. Using 2 tablespoons, carefully scoop one batter-coated shrimp into one spoon, and with the other spoon, push the mixture into the hot oil (be careful not to splash the oil). For best results, fry no more than four beignets at a time. Using a slotted spoon, turn the beignets to cook 1 minute per side, until puffy and light brown all over. With a slotted spoon, remove the beignets from the oil and let drain on the prepared plate.

To serve, season with salt and accompany with the sauce.

SMOKED FISH SPREAD WITH BUTTERMILK CRACKERS

Makes 4 cups spread and about 24 crackers

Every time Slade and I visit my mom in St. Petersburg, Florida, our first plan of action is a visit to Ted Peter's Smoked Fish near the beach. At the open air bar, we nosh on the smoked mullet dip amidst the mingling aromas of ocean breezes and the smoke-house out back. At MiLa, we smoke redfish for our version and make buttermilk crackers from scratch. But if homemade crackers seem daunting, just eat it like we do at Ted Peter's, on saltines with a dash of hot sauce.

1 pound redfish fillets, skinned, boned, and diced
    (mullet or tuna are good substitutes)
2 tablespoons Dijon mustard
4 large egg yolks
2 tablespoons freshly squeezed lemon juice
2 cups canola or other neutral vegetable oil
1 tablespoon capers, drained
1 tablespoon Worcesteshire sauce
1 tablespoon hot sauce (we like Crystal's)
1 tablespoon extra-virgin olive oil
3 tablespoons garlic confit (page 221)
6 cornichons, plus 1 tablespoon of their brine
1/2 teaspoon sea salt
1/2 teaspoon freshly ground black pepper
Buttermilk Crackers, for accompaniment
    (recipe follows)

To smoke the redfish, in a pot large enough to hold a metal colander, place 1/2 cup hickory chips in the center of the bottom of the pot. Place the diced fish in the colander and season with salt and pepper. Place the colander in the pot and cover the pot tightly with aluminum foil. Place the pot on the stove over high heat and let cook until a steady smoke begins to spew out of the pot. Once you see the smoke, decrease the heat to low and smoke for 5 minutes. Turn off the heat and let the fish smoke for another 5 minutes. Remove the foil and let the fish cool.

To make the spread, in a blender, combine the mustard, egg yolks, and lemon juice and blend on low speed until just combined. With the blender on low speed, slowly drizzle in the canola oil in a steady stream until a thick mayonnaise is formed. Add the capers, Worcestershire sauce, hot sauce, olive oil, confit, cornichons and brine, salt, pepper, and the smoked fish. Blend on high speed until smooth, stopping to scrape down the sides of the blender when necessary.

Serve chilled, accompanied by Buttermilk Crackers. Keeps for up to 1 week refrigerated.

BUTTERMILK CRACKERS

2 cups all-purpose flour

1 teaspoon baking powder

1 teaspoon kosher salt

1/2 teaspoon freshly ground black pepper

1/2 teaspoon fresh thyme leaves (no stems)

2 tablespoons cold unsalted butter, cut in
    1/4-inch dice

1/3 to 1/2 cup cold buttermilk

In a large bowl, whisk together the flour, baking powder, salt, and pepper until they are evenly distributed. Add the butter to the dry ingredients and, using a pastry cutter, work the butter into the flour until the butter pieces are the size of lentils. Add the buttermilk. Using a wooden spoon, stir the mixture until all the liquid is incorporated and a dough begins to form.

Turn out the dough onto a lightly floured work surface and knead the dough back and forth until it is nice and smooth, about 1 minute. Wrap the dough tightly in plastic wrap and chill it in the refrigerator for at least 30 minutes.

Meanwhile, preheat the oven to 350°F.

Place the chilled dough on a lightly floured work surface. Using a rolling pin, roll the dough in all directions until very thin, about 1/16 inch thick. Using a fork, pierce the dough to make holes about 1/2 inch apart. Using a knife or a pizza cutter, cut the dough into 2-inch squares.

Place the crackers on a nonstick baking sheet and bake until they are crisp and lightly browned on the edges, about 15 minutes.

PIMIENTO CHEESE CROQUETTES

MAKES 50 CROQUETTES

We boldly served this Southern deli staple where it had not been before: as bread service in a New York City restaurant. This retro spread of Cheddar cheese, mayo, roasted peppers, and grated onion has made quite the comeback on menus around the country. In order to make it a more elegant party food, we wrap little balls in panko and deep fry them, resulting in crunchy delicious cheesy bites. Eat your leftovers the traditonal way, as a spread between two slices of white bread.

1 large red bell pepper

1/2 teaspoon extra-virgin olive oil

1/2 cup pecans

10 ounces sharp Cheddar cheese, grated

1/2 cup homemade mayonnaise (page 221)

1/4 cup minced onion

2 tablespoons thinly sliced green onion, white and green parts

2 teaspoons Worcestershire sauce

11/2 teaspoons champagne vinegar

1 teaspoon finely minced garlic

1/2 teaspoon salt

1/2 teaspoon freshly ground black pepper

Canola or other neutral vegetable oil, for frying

1 cup all-purpose flour

2 large eggs, lightly beaten

1 cup whole milk

2 cups panko (Japanese bread crumbs)

Preheat the oven to 350°F.

To roast the red bell pepper, coat the pepper in olive oil, place on a baking sheet, and roast until charred on all sides and soft when touched, about 30 minutes.

To toast the pecans, place the pecans on a second baking sheet and lightly toast them in the oven for 7 minutes. Let the pecans cool, then chop them finely and reserve.

To prepare the roasted pepper, remove the pepper from the baking sheet, place in a small plastic bag, and seal tightly. After 10 minutes, carefully remove the pepper from the bag. With the back of a spoon or with a knife, scrape off the charred skin from the pepper. Halve the pepper and remove all the seeds and the stem. Chop the pepper finely and reserve until needed.

To form the cheese balls, place the grated cheese in a food processor fitted with the metal blade and pulse until lentil-size pieces form. Combine the cheese in a large bowl along with the red pepper, pecans, mayonnaise, onion, green onion, Worcestershire sauce, vinegar, garlic, salt, and pepper. Using a wooden spoon or plastic spatula, combine all of the ingredients together to form a smooth paste.

For each cheese ball, place about 1 tablespoon of the mixture between the palms of your hands and roll quickly to form a ball about the size of a ping-pong ball. Repeat until all of the cheese mixture is used. Place all of the pimiento cheese balls on a baking sheet and refrigerate for 30 minutes.

Fill a heavy, deep saucepan with at least 6 inches of oil. Heat the oil over medium-high heat until it registers 340°F on a deep-fry thermometer.

Meanwhile set up a breading station: Place the flour in a bowl. In a second bowl, make an egg wash by whisking the eggs and milk together; set aside until needed. In a third bowl, place the panko. After the pimiento cheese balls have chilled, bread them in this order: dust in flour, then drop in the egg wash, then coat in the panko crumbs.

Place the breaded pimiento cheese balls on a baking sheet and refrigerate until you are ready to fry them.

To fry the croquettes, drop them in the hot oil in small batches and fry them until they are golden brown and begin to float, about 2 minutes.

Serve them right away and as we do, in a linen-lined bread basket.

SHRIMP SAUSAGE WRAPS WITH LIME DIPPING SAUCE

MAKES ABOUT 20 PIECES

Vietnamese cuisine is probably not the first thing that comes to mind when one thinks of New Orleans. Around the end of the Vietnam War, many refugees from that country settled here, drawn by the familiar climate and the strong Catholic community. Many of them are employed by the local fishing industry, while others have opened traditional restaurants. On our days off, we often dine at our favorite Vietnamese restaurant on the Westbank, Tan Dinh, where the food is always fresh and vibrant. This canapé reflects those light, clean flavors we just can't get enough of.

SHRIMP SAUSAGES

1 pound (21/25 count) shrimp, peeled and deveined

2 large egg whites

1/2 teaspoon ground white pepper

1/2 teaspoon cayenne pepper

1/2 teaspoon paprika

1 teaspoon chopped fresh ginger

1 teaspoon chopped garlic

1 teaspoon fine sea salt

1 tablespoon thinly sliced green onion, white and green parts

1 tablespoon heavy cream

LIME DIPPING SAUCE

1 teaspoon chopped garlic

1 tablespoon pepper vinegar (page 222)

2 tablespoons sugar

2 tablespoons Vietnamese fish sauce

3 tablespoons freshly squeezed lime juice

1 large carrot, peeled and julienned

Leaves from 1 bunch cilantro

Small Bibb lettuce leaves, for serving

To make the sausages, using a food processor fitted with the metal blade, puree the shrimp until it becomes a smooth paste. Add the egg whites and pulse until well incorporated. Using a rubber spatula, remove the shrimp mixture from the food processor and transfer to a bowl. Add the white pepper, cayenne, paprika, ginger, garlic, salt, green onion, and cream and mix thoroughly.

For each sausage, place a 12-inch-square piece of plastic wrap on your work surface. Put 3 tablespoons of the sausage mixture in the center of the plastic wrap. Fold the bottom corners of the plastic wrap up to touch the top corners of the plastic wrap, forming a rectangle. Pull the plastic wrap back until it is tight around the sausage mixture, forming a cigar shape about 1/2 inch in diameter. Using your fingertips, tuck and roll the sausage forward and twist the ends of the plastic wrap tightly closed. Tie off the twisted ends of the sausages with kitchen twine or unflavored dental floss. Repeat with the remaining sausage mixture. You will have about 20 pieces.

Half fill a large saucepan with water and bring to a boil over high heat. Fill a large bowl with ice water. Poach the sausages in three batches (still in the plastic wrap) for 3 minutes. Place in the ice bath to chill completely, then unwrap and set aside on a plate. This can be done 1 day ahead.

To make the sauce, whisk together the garlic, pepper vinegar, sugar, fish sauce, and lime juice in a small bowl.

Slice the sausages into 1/4-inch slices. To serve, wrap slices of sausage in lettuce leaves, garnish with julienned carrot and cilantro leaves, and drizzle with sauce.

VENISON AND CHEDDAR BISCUITS

MAKES 36 PIECES

These biscuits remind me of deer hunting with my dad in Mississippi. When as a boy I was too small to climb up into the deer stand by myself, my dad would kneel down, have me wrap my arms around his neck, and carry me up like a little monkey. On those cold winter afternoons, I had my dad all to myself in the woods. Trekking back home, we would listen to the owls hoot as the sun went down. That comfort comes back to me every time I make these biscuits.

4 cups all-purpose flour

1 1/2 tablespoons baking powder

2 teaspoons salt

3/4 cup unsalted butter, cold, cut in small dice

12 ounces sharp Vermont white Cheddar, grated

14 ounces venison sausage, crumbled

1 cup whole milk

1 large egg

1/2 cup heavy cream, for brushing the tops

Butter, for serving (optional)

Preheat the oven to 350°F.

In a large bowl, whisk together the flour, baking powder, and salt. Add the butter, cheese, and sausage and working quickly, rub all the ingredients together with your fingertips until the butter is the size of small peas. In a separate bowl, whisk together the milk and egg. Add the wet ingredients to the dry ingredients and bring them together with your hands just until the dough comes together.

Turn the mixture out onto a lightly floured work surface and work the dough by carefully kneading it, just until the dough becomes nice and smooth, about 10 times. Be careful not to overwork it or the biscuits will be tough.

Lightly flour the work surface again, if necessary, and roll the dough out with a rolling pin until it is 1 inch thick. Using a 1 1/2-inch round cutter, cut out the biscuits and place them on a nonstick baking sheet, about 1 1/2 inches apart.

Using a pastry brush, lightly brush the tops of the biscuits with the cream. Bake until golden brown on the top, about 15 minutes.

Serve immediately with butter, if desired.

LIMA BEAN DIP WITH PITA CHIPS

Makes 4 cups

At MiLa, we serve lima bean puree with our cornbread and sweet potato rolls. Our customers constantly ask for the recipe and are surprised at how few ingredients it contains. This puree is very versatile. We have served it as an elegant accompaniment to lamb, and it is also quite nice as a cold dip for crudités. Here is it a great stand-in for hummus, served with purchased or homemade pita chips. Keep the leftover dip in your fridge for up to two weeks for a quick snack or sandwich spread.

1 pound dried lima beans

4 cups water

1 carrot

1 onion

1 stalk celery

1 head garlic, top cut off

1 bay leaf

1/4 cup pepper vinegar (page 222)

1/2 cup unsalted butter, diced

1 1/2 teaspoons fine sea salt

1/2 teaspoon ground white pepper

1 tablespoon extra-virgin olive oil

1/2 teaspoon Creole spice (page 222)

Pita Chips

1 bag pita bread

Canola or other neutral vegetable oil, for frying

Sea salt

To make the dip, place the lima beans, water, carrot, onion, celery, garlic, and bay leaf in a large saucepot over medium-high heat. Bring the mixture to a simmmer, and using a ladle, continue to skim the scum off of the surface for about 5 minutes. Once all of the scum is removed, decrease the heat to low and simmmer until the beans are easily smashed between two fingers, about 1 1/2 hours. Remove the carrot, onion, celery, bay leaf, and garlic and discard them. Stir in the pepper vinegar.

Put one-third of the beans and cooking liquid and one-third of the diced butter in a blender. Before turning on the machine, be sure the lid is tightly secured and covered with a towel to prevent the hot mixture from escaping. Blend the mixture first on slow speed, gradually increasing the speed to high until it's a smooth puree. Transfer the puree from the blender to a large bowl, using a rubber spatula to scrape the sides of the jar. Repeat this process twice more until all of your beans are pureed with butter. Whisk the salt and white pepper into the puree until fully incorporated. Place the puree in a serving bowl and top it with the olive oil and Creole spice.

If you decide to make your own pita chips, fill a heavy, deep saucepan with at least 6 inches of oil. Heat the oil over medium-high heat until it registers 350°F on a deep-fry thermometer.

Line a tray with paper towels and have nearby. While the oil is heating, halve each pita bread horizontally, then cut each half into eight wedges. Fry the chips in batches until brown and crispy on all sides, about 1 minute. With a slotted spoon, transfer the chips from the oil to the prepared tray and lightly season with sea salt.

Serve the pita chips along side the lima bean puree.

OYSTERS ROCKEFELLER "DECONSTRUCTED"

SERVES 4

Slade and I created this dish in 2003 for the opening of Jack's Luxury Oyster Bar. We wanted to re-invent this iconic New Orleans dish, which, in our opinion, had seen better days. Using techniques we had learned in New York City kitchens, like poaching seafood in butter, determining the essential elements of the dish, and highlighting their singularity, we think we helped restore oysters Rockefeller to its former glory. The gently poached oysters rest on a bed of brown-butter spinach topped with crunchy bacon and a whisper of grated licorice root. We use Mississippi and Louisiana Gulf oysters, but an East Coast variety such as Blue Point is a great choice as well. The Vines family philosophers, my sister Jennifer and her husband Jason, loved the nod to the philosophical theory of deconstruction in the name.

4 thin slices bacon

2 cups unsalted butter

12 ounces baby spinach

2 cloves garlic, peeled and crushed

2 shallots, finely diced

Salt and freshly ground black pepper

2 tablespoons water

1 lemon, thinly sliced

20 medium oysters, freshly shucked (see headnote)

1 stick licorice root (see Sources, page 223)

Line a plate with paper towels. In a large skillet over medium heat, cook the bacon until it is browned and crispy, about 5 minutes. Transfer the bacon to the prepared plate and let cool, then chop it finely and reserve.

To prepare the spinach mixture, heat 1/2 cup of the butter in a deep skillet over medium-high heat until it begins to brown. Add the spinach, garlic, and shallots, and season well with salt and pepper. Cook until the greens are just wilted, about 1 minute, being careful not to cook too long. Transfer the spinach to a colander to drain. Remove and discard the crushed garlic and finely chop the spinach. Set aside.

To make the butter sauce, cut the remaining 1 1/2 cups butter into 1-inch cubes. Heat the water in a small saucepan until simmering. Decrease the heat and whisk in the butter pieces, one by one, whisking constantly and emulsifying the butter into the water. Once the butter is incorporated, the result is a smooth, velvety sauce. Turn off the heat, add the lemon slices, and steep for about 15 minutes. Season with salt to taste. This should be kept warm on top of the stove (not on direct heat) until ready to use.

To assemble the dish, bring the butter sauce to a simmer. Rewarm the spinach mixture over low heat in a small saucepan and place it in neat piles in small serving spoons. Drop the oysters in the simmering butter and poach them until they are warm and the edges begin to curl slightly, about 30 seconds. Transfer the oysters with a slotted spoon to a small bowl. Place an oyster on each pile of spinach. Spoon a small amount of butter sauce onto each oyster. Top each with chopped bacon. Finely grate licorice root on top and serve.

Note: Instead of licorice root, you can add 1 teaspoon of licorice-flavored liqueur, such as Pernod or Herbsaint, to your butter sauce for a similar flavor.

SALADS

SALADS

WHEN I WAS A KID, one of the most stressful questions I faced when we went out to dinner was figuring out what kind of dressing I wanted on my salad. If it wasn't smothered in my dressing of choice and served with Captain's Wafers on the side, I did not want it. Having no idea what lettuce actually tasted like, I was lost for many years.

I didn't feel any different until some years later in culinary school at Johnson and Wales in Providence, Rhode Island. In my garde manger class, I was amazed at the varieties of lettuce in the world and the techniques one used to create dressings and vinaigrettes from scratch. My family shopped at the local Piggly Wiggly, so I thought that all salads came from iceberg.

When building a great salad you absolutely must choose the freshest of lettuces. If the greens look just okay, not great, do yourself a favor and start the meal with a soup or other first course, not a salad. A great salad may look easy when it's put in front of you, but it is actually one of the hardest dishes to prepare well. It requires a perfect balance of many things: just enough dressing, precise amounts of salt and pepper, a delicate touch of the hands, and two tools—the salad spinner and a Japanese mandoline. Also, once made, a salad should be enjoyed right away. In my opinion, no one can make them better than my Allison.

CUCUMBER AND GOAT CHEESE "CANNELLONI" WITH MARINATED TOMATOES

SERVES 4

This delicious salad is so easy to make—and visually stunning. Strips of cucumber are rolled around tangy goat cheese to simulate cannelloni pasta, then garnished with bright cherry tomatoes, baby basil, and a deep balsamic reduction. Perfect for a summer lunch and it will garner you the envy of your "chef-y" friends.

1/4 cup extra-virgin olive oil

Sprig of thyme (leaves only)

10 cherry tomatoes, halved

1/4 cup balsamic vinegar

8 ounces fresh goat cheese

1 tablespoon heavy cream

1 teaspoon freshly ground black pepper

2 English cucumbers

Fleur de sel (French sea salt), for garnish

12 small fresh basil leaves, for garnish

To make the marinated tomatoes, combine the olive oil, thyme leaves, and cherry tomatoes in a small bowl and let them marinate for about 30 minutes. In a small saucepan, reduce the balsamic vinegar over medium heat, keeping a close eye not to burn it, until it is syrupy. Set aside.

To make the goat cheese mixture, in a small bowl, using a rubber spatula, mix the goat cheese with the cream and pepper until it is smooth and creamy. Divide the mixture into eight equal portions and roll each with your hands into a log shape.

Cut the ends off of the English cucumbers (as they are thin-skinned, they don't need to

be peeled, but peel the cucumbers if using a thicker-skinned variety). Halve both cucumbers crosswise at their midsections, so you end up with 4 equal-size pieces of cucumber. With a mandoline, slice each cucumber lengthwise into ribbons about 1/8 inch thick. For each "cannelloni," place one cucumber ribbon on the work surface. Lay one slice of cucumber down, then another slice of cucumber halfway down. Repeat two more "shingles" for four slices total.

Place one log of goat cheese mixture on the left of the shingled cucumbers and roll it to the right until you have a cannelloni shape with the seam on the bottom; you end up with a cucumber-covered log. Repeat with the remaining sliced cucumbers and goat cheese logs. You should end up with eight logs.

To serve, place two "cannelloni" in the center of each plate. Top each serving with five marinated tomato halves and a sprinkling of fleur de sel. Using a spoon, garnish the plate with a circle of balsamic reduction around the "cannelloni." Garnish each plate with a few small basil leaves.

CREOLE-SPICED SHRIMP SALAD

SERVES 4

This island-inspired summer salad keeps your mouth entertained with hot and cold temperatures. The spicy shrimp are tamed by the cool avocado and the vinegary heart of palm. We love to pair it with a citrusy Portuguese vinho verde. Because of its sturdy nature, this salad is a great option for a Fourth of July buffet. Just don't expect any leftovers.

1 head romaine lettuce

DRESSING

1/2 teaspoon sugar

1/4 teaspoon salt

1/4 teaspoon freshly ground black pepper

1 teaspoon Dijon mustard

Grated zest and juice of 1 lemon

2 tablespoon champagne vinegar

1 tablespoon minced shallots

2 tablespoons extra-virgin olive oil

SHRIMP SALAD

1 tablespoon extra-virgin olive oil

20 (16/20 count; about 1 pound) shrimp, peeled and
deveined

1 tablespoon Creole spice (page 222)

16 cherry tomatoes, halved

12 canned hearts of palm, drained and cut in
1/2-inch dice

1 ripe avocado, quartered, pitted, and peeled

2 ounces fresh chives, cut in 2-inch lengths,
for garnish

To prepare the lettuce, pick away all of the tough outer green leaves of the head of romaine. Break apart the lettuce hearts into individual leaves. Place the leaves in a bath of clean cold water to rinse away any grit; dry in a salad spinner. Keep the lettuce leaves in the refrigerator in a plastic bag until you are ready to serve the salad.

To make the dressing, in a large bowl, whisk together the sugar, salt, pepper, mustard, lemon zest and juice, vinegar, shallots, and olive oil until thoroughly combined. Reserve.

To cook the shrimp, heat a large sauté pan with the olive oil over high heat until it is barely smoking. Season the shrimp liberally with Creole spice and add them to the hot pan. Cook the shrimp for 2 minutes, then flip them and cook on the other side for an additional 2 minutes. Remove from the pan.

Place the hot shrimp in the bowl of dressing along with the tomatoes, hearts of palm, and the crisped romaine leaves and toss all together until everything is coated well. Slice each avocado quarter into four slices.

To serve, place the romaine leaves down first on a large platter, then top with the tomatoes, hearts of palm, shrimp, and sliced avocado. Spoon the remaining vinaigrette over the salad and garnish with the chives.

GREEN TOMATO SALAD WITH BLUE CHEESE DRESSING AND CRISPY SHALLOTS

SERVES 4

The amazing green apple flavor of green tomatoes isn't quite discernible when they are served fried, as is traditional. We let them shine in their natural state with this salad, paired with a sturdy green like frisée and a fruity blue cheese. Be sure to use a good quality blue. One of our favorites is the French Fourme d'Ambert. Spanish Valdéon is another great choice. We do still utilize the fryer, though, for some crispy shallots to add a bit of crunch.

BLUE CHEESE DRESSING

1/2 cup buttermilk

1/4 cup homemade mayonnaise (page 221)

1/4 cup sour cream

1 teaspoon honey

1 teaspoon apple cider vinegar

1/4 teaspoon chopped garlic

1 teaspoon chopped fresh chives

1/8 teaspoon cayenne pepper

1/8 teaspoon salt

1/8 teaspoon freshly ground black pepper

4 ounces blue cheese, crumbled, about 1/2 cup

GREEN TOMATO SALAD

Canola or other neutral vegetable oil, for frying

2 heads frisée (curly endive)

2 large, firm green tomatoes

4 shallots

1/2 cup Wondra flour (see sidebar on page 150)

3/4 teaspoon salt

1/2 teaspoon coarsely cracked black pepper, for seasoning (optional)

To make the dressing, in a large bowl, whisk together the buttermilk, mayonnaise, sour cream, honey, vinegar, garlic, chives, cayenne, salt, and black pepper. Fold in the blue cheese and chill until needed.

Fill a heavy, deep saucepan with at least 6 inches of oil. Heat the oil over medium-high heat until it registers 350°F on a deep-fry thermometer.

To prepare the salad, with kitchen scissors, trim off and discard all of the dark green edges from the frisée. Separate the tender yellow heart of the frisée into small clusters and wash and dry them in a salad spinner. Reserve.

Remove the cores from the green tomatoes using a small knife or a melon baller. Cut the tomatoes into 1/2-inch dice. Reserve.

Line a plate or tray with paper towels and have nearby. Slice the shallots on a mandoline into paper-thin rings. In a bowl, mix together the flour with 1/2 teaspoon of the salt. Add the shallot rings to the bowl, coating them well in the flour mixture. Transfer the shallots to a wire strainer and shake off all of the excess flour. Place the shallots in the hot oil and fry until golden and crispy, about 1 minute. Transfer them to the prepared plate and season again with the remaining 1/4 teaspoon salt.

To finish the salad, toss the tomatoes and frisée with the chilled dressing. Top the salad with the fried shallots and, if desired, the coarsely cracked pepper.

Serve right away.

SPRING VEGETABLE SALAD WITH LEMON VINAIGRETTE

SERVES 4

It isn't hard to find inspiration in the springtime, when crisp, tender green vegetables flood the market. In this salad, we think the more green the better and use grassy asparagus, sweet green peas, and flowery broccoli florets. Be sure to pay attention when blanching, as there is a brief window of time when the perfect al dente is reached. Combine your perfectly cooked veggies with peppery radishes, a bright vinaigrette, and shavings of fruity Parmesan and awaken your taste buds after that long cold winter.

DRESSING

1 shallot, minced

1 clove garlic, minced

2 teaspoons honey

Grated zest and juice of 1 lemon

2 teaspoons champagne vinegar

1/4 cup light olive oil

1/2 teaspoon fine sea salt

1/4 teaspoon coarsely ground black pepper

VEGETABLE SALAD

1 bunch green asparagus

1 medium head broccoli

1/2 cup shelled fresh green peas

1 head Bibb lettuce (preferably hydroponic)

4 red radishes

4-ounce wedge Parmesan cheese, for shaving

To make the dressing, combine all the ingredients in a mason jar and shake well. Chill until needed.

To prepare the vegetables, bring a large saucepan filled with 4 quarts water and 1/4 cup kosher salt to a boil.

Meanwhile, for the asparagus, trim off the lower third of the stems and discard. Halve the asparagus diagonally. For the broccoli, using a small knife, cut off the florets from the stem (halve the florets, if necessary, so they are all in bite-size pieces).

Line a baking sheet with paper towels and have ready. Set a colander in a bowl of ice water and have ready. Once the water is boiling, blanch each green vegetable separately, transferring each with a slotted or wire mesh spoon to the colander in the ice water bath after blanching, and letting the water in the pot return to a boil between each one. Blanch in this order: the peas, boiling for 1 minute; then the broccoli, boiling for 1 1/2 minutes; then the asparagus, cooking until al dente, 1 to 2 minutes, depending on the thickness of the stalks. Remove the blanched vegetables from the ice water and let them dry on the prepared baking sheet.

Separate the leaves of Bibb lettuce, discarding the large, tough outer leaves. Wash and dry completely. Shave the radishes into paper-thin slices with a mandoline.

To assemble the salad, dress all of the vegetables and lettuce lightly with the vinaigrette and place in a bowl. Using a vegetable peeler or mandoline, shave the Parmesan over the salad to garnish.

GREEN BEAN AND TOMATO SALAD WITH CORNBREAD CROUTONS

SERVES 4

You can prepare this summer salad ahead of time, making it perfect for picnics or barbecues. It is a great side dish for grilled meats or fried chicken, but could certainly stand on its own as a light lunch. Our farmer, Luther, brings us an assortment of green beans in the summer—such as Chinese long beans, romano beans, and rattlesnack beans—all of which add different colors and textures to the salad.

DRESSING

1 teaspoon Dijon mustard

1 teaspoon honey

1 tablespoon minced shallots

2 tablespoons red wine vinegar

1/4 teaspoon sea salt

1/4 teaspoon freshly ground black pepper

1/4 cup light olive oil

SALAD

2 cups Shallot Cornbread (page 29), cut in
　　1/2-inch dice

1 pound fresh green beans (any variety or an
　　assortment), ends trimmed

1 pint cherry or grape tomatoes, halved

1 cup flat-leaf parsley leaves

1/4 teaspoon sea salt

1/4 teaspoon coarsely ground black pepper

To make the dressing, in a small bowl, whisk together the mustard, honey, shallots, vinegar, salt, and pepper until smooth. Drizzle in the oil in a slow and steady stream while whisking to emulsify the vinaigrette. Reserve.

To make the croutons, preheat the oven to 350°F. Arrange the diced cornbread in an even layer on a small baking sheet and toast in the oven, stirring occasionally, until golden brown, about 15 minutes. Remove from the oven and let cool.

To cook the green beans, bring a large saucepan filled with 4 quarts water and 1/4 cup kosher salt to a boil. Line a baking sheet with paper towels and have ready. Set a colander in a bowl of ice water and have ready.

Once the water has reached a boil, cook the green beans until they are bright green and just cooked through, 2 to 3 minutes. With a slotted or wire-mesh spoon, transfer the beans to the colander in the ice water bath to cool. Once cool, drain on the prepared baking sheet.

To finish the salad, toss the green beans, tomatoes, croutons, and parsley with the vinaigrette. Season with the salt and pepper and serve.

ARUGULA SALAD WITH ASIAN PEAR AND SHEEP'S MILK CHEESE

SERVES 4

At the restaurant, fall menus are among our favorites to create. After a hot, brutal New Orleans summer, we start to see the people of the city smile a little easier as the weather cools down. Another welcome sight is the abundance of produce from our farmer, Luther. One of our most coveted ingredients is his arugula. Tender, spicy, sweet, and vibrant green, it is everything arugula should be. This salad presents the perfect stage for this star ingredient. With the crunch of pecans, sweetness of the pear, and the creamy, funky richness of the cheese, your friends will think you are a star, too.

1 tablespoon honey

1 tablespoon Dijon mustard

1 tablespoon apple cider vinegar

1 tablespoon canola oil or light olive oil

8 ounces baby arugula

1 Asian pear, peeled and very thinly sliced

1/2 teaspoon fine sea salt

4 ounces sheep's milk cheese (we use Thomasville Tomme), sliced paper thin

1/2 cup Candied Pecans (recipe follows)

In a small bowl, whisk together the honey, mustard, and vinegar. Add the oil in a small, steady stream while whisking to emulsify the vinaigrette.

In a separate mixing bowl, toss the arugula, pear, and salt with the dressing until everything is nicely coated.

To serve, place the dressed salad on a plate and top with the sheep cheese and candied pecans.

CANDIED PECANS

1 large egg white

1/8 teaspoon cayenne pepper

1/8 teaspoon ground cinnamon

1/4 teaspoon salt

1/2 cup packed brown sugar

1 tablespoon honey

2 cups pecan halves

Preheat the oven to 300°F.

In a large bowl, whisk the egg white until it is frothy. Add the cayenne, cinnamon, salt, and brown sugar and whisk until combined. Add the honey and the pecans and toss all together until well coated.

Spread the pecans evenly on a baking sheet and bake until they have a frosted look and are dry to the touch, about 20 minutes. Stored in an airtight container, the pecans will keep for up to 2 weeks.

CABBAGE AND DRIED FIG SALAD WITH GARLIC VINAIGRETTE

SERVES 4

This sturdy salad is prepared like a winter version of coleslaw. You must season your cabbage and allow the water to seep out, tenderizing it before you combine it with the other ingredients. But the most important thing for the success of this dish is to make sure your pine nuts are not Chinese! Both Slade and I came down with a terrible affliction where everything we put in our mouth tasted bitter for weeks. It took us quite some time to figure out the cause was Chinese pine nuts. Thankfully it did not permanently alter our palates, but it did give us a renewed appreciation for those other tastes of sweet, sour, salty, and umami; all of which are found in this recipe.

1 head savoy cabbage

1 1/2 teaspoons fine sea salt

1 teaspoon sugar

1 head garlic, roasted (see sidebar)

1/2 teaspoon chopped garlic

1/2 teaspoon Dijon mustard

2 tablespoons honey

3 tablespoons sherry vinegar

1/2 teaspoon freshly ground black pepper

1/2 cup light olive oil

1 head radicchio

8 ounces dried figs (or dried prunes or dates)

1/2 cup pine nuts, toasted

Halve and core the cabbage and slice each half into thin ribbons (julienne). In a small bowl, toss the julienned cabbage with 1 teaspoon of the salt and the sugar, coating it evenly. Place the cabbage in a colander placed over a bowl and let it sit for at least 1 hour.

Remove the garlic cloves from the head of roasted garlic by gently squeezing the base of the garlic head. Smash the cloves of garlic with a bottom of a spoon to make a smooth paste. In a small bowl, whisk together the garlic paste with the chopped garlic, mustard, honey, vinegar, the remaining 1/2 teaspoon salt, and pepper until well mixed. Drizzle all of the oil into the bowl in a slow, steady stream while whisking to emulsify the vinaigrette. Reserve.

Halve the radicchio and slice each half into thin ribbons (julienne) like the cabbage. Once the cabbage has softened, place it in a mixing bowl with the radicchio, dried figs, and the dressing.

Toss the salad to coat it evenly with dressing and place in a serving dish. Top with the toasted pine nuts and serve.

ROASTED GARLIC

Preheat the oven to 350°F. With a sharp knife, trim the top off a head of garlic. Set the garlic in the middle of a piece of foil and pour 1 teaspoon of extra-virgin olive oil over the top. Wrap the foil tightly around the garlic, place it on a baking sheet, and bake for 1 hour.

SCALLOP SALAD WITH GRAPEFRUIT AND ROMAINE HEARTS

SERVES 4

Wintertime in Louisiana brings a bounty of citrus to roadside stands and markets. While navel oranges and satsumas are common, newer varieties to the area include Meyer lemons, blood oranges, and ruby red grapefruit—our personal favorite. Their bittersweet flavor is a sophisticated match for roasted scallops and their briny juices.

DRESSING

1/4 cup freshly squeezed ruby red grapefruit juice

1 tablespoon minced shallots

1 teaspoon minced garlic

1 teaspoon honey

1 teaspoon champagne vinegar

1/4 cup extra-virgin olive oil

1/8 teaspoon salt

1/8 teaspoon coarsely ground black pepper

SCALLOP SALAD

1 tablespoon extra-virgin olive oil

12 medium sea scallops, preferably dry-packed

1/4 teaspoon salt

1/4 teaspoon freshly ground black pepper

2 large romaine hearts, cut into thin ribbons

1 ruby red grapefruit, peeled and segmented

2 tablespoons toasted sunflower seeds, for garnish

To make the dressing, in a small bowl, whisk together the grapfruit juice, shallots, garlic, honey, vinegar, olive oil, salt, and pepper. Chill until needed.

To prepare the scallops, heat a large sauté pan over high heat until smoking; add the olive oil. Season the scallops on both sides with salt and pepper. Decrease the heat to medium and carefully add the scallops to the pan, evenly spaced apart. Sear them on each side until a golden brown crust is formed and the scallops are slightly firm to the touch, about 2 minutes per side. Remove the scallops from the pan to a plate; reserve.

To assemble the salad, in a medium bowl, toss the romaine hearts and the grapefruit segments in the dressing.

To serve, divide the salad among four plates and top each with three scallops. Finish with a sprinkle of sunflower seeds.

SOUPS

SOUP HAS SUCH A POWER to evoke warm and loving memories. Like when Mom made chicken soup when we were sick, or rainy day tomato soup enjoyed with grilled cheese. In addition to those soups triggered by great memories, our soups are also often inspired by a plentiful crop of vegetables at their peak, which we enhance with the addition of garnishes.

A crispy garnish, such as croutons, or a textural addition of a grain, adds heartiness, while a cold and creamy garnish like crème fraîche or goat cheese cools down heat and spice.

The addition of seafood, such as caviar, lobster, or poached oysters, adds elegance. Fresh herbs add vibrance to your soup, and seasonal pairings, such as summertime vegetables with basil or winter beans with rosemary, always work. Although sometimes all you need to make a good memory is a warm French baguette torn by hand and enjoyed with every last drop in your bowl.

CURRIED SQUASH AND CRAWFISH SOUP

SERVES 8

An overabundance of yellow squash in the summertime is put to good use in this Indian-inspired soup. Curry and squash are great partners, the squash providing body while the curry provides a much needed flavor boost. The crème fraîche cools off the spice and the addition of crawfish shows the kindred nature of New Orleans and Indian cuisines.

1/2 cup unsalted butter, diced

1 cup shallots, julienned

2 tablespoons thinly sliced garlic

1 teaspoon fine sea salt

1/2 teaspoon ground white pepper

2 teaspoons good-quality yellow curry powder

1 bay leaf

Sprig of thyme

1/2 cup white wine

1/4 cup heavy cream

4 cups vegetable stock (page 220)

2 pounds yellow squash, cut in large dice

1 pound crawfish tails, backs removed

1 cup crème fraîche (page 221)

Small fresh basil leaves, for garnish (optional)

Melt the butter in a large saucepan over medium-high heat. Add the shallots, garlic, salt, white pepper, curry powder, bay leaf, and thyme and decrease the heat to medium. Cook, stirring frequently, until the shallots and garlic are soft and translucent. Add the white wine and cook until the liquid is reduced by half. Add the cream, stock, and squash and cook until the squash is soft, about 30 minutes.

Remove the pot from the heat and let the soup cool for at least 20 minutes.

Puree the soup in a blender on medium speed in two batches. Before turning on the machine, be sure the lid is tightly secured and covered with a towel to prevent the hot mixture from escaping. Puree the soup until it is nice and smooth, finishing on high speed to ensure its smoothness.

Before serving, reheat the soup in a saucepan, add the crawfish tails, and heat the soup until the crawfish tails are warm (they're small and they heat quickly). Garnish the soup with crème fraîche and basil leaves.

BUTTERNUT SQUASH SOUP WITH SPICED CRÈME FRAÎCHE

SERVES 8

We have yet to come across a person who does not like butternut squash soup. Even staunch vegetable haters fall for it. (Maybe its sweet richness makes them think that it can't be healthy.) When it is on the menu at the restaurant, probably eighty percent of our customers order it, leaving the cooks to complain about how much they have to make. And if you peek through the kitchen doors, you will undoubtedly see one of us with a steaming hot bowl of it in our own grubby hands.

3 pounds butternut squash

1 tablespoon extra-virgin olive oil

2 tablespoons unsalted butter

2 cups sliced shallots

1/3 cup smashed garlic cloves

1 teaspoon fine sea salt

1/2 teaspoon ground white pepper

1 spice purse (1 bay leaf, 1 thyme sprig, 1 star anise, 4 whole peppercorns wrapped in cheesecloth and tied closed with kitchen string)

1/2 cup white wine

1 tablespoon sugar (optional)

8 cups vegetable stock (page 220)

1/2 cup heavy cream

1/4 teaspoon ground cinnamon

1/4 teaspoon freshly grated nutmeg

1/4 teaspoon freshly grated licorice root (optional; see Sources, page 223 and Note, page 61)

Spiced Crème Fraîche, for accompaniment (recipe follows)

To roast the squash, preheat the oven to 350°F.

With a vegetable peeler, remove the skin from the squash. Carefully cut the squash in half lengthwise. Scoop out and discard the seeds. Place the squash on a baking sheet and drizzle with the olive oil. Roast the squash until it is soft and caramelized, about 30 minutes.

To make the soup, in a large soup pot over medium heat, melt the butter and then add the shallots, garlic, salt, white pepper, and spice purse. Cook until the shallots are soft and translucent, about 3 minutes. Add the wine and cook until the mixture is reduced by half, about 3 minutes. Add the squash, sugar, stock, and cream. Cook until all of the flavors meld together, 20 to 30 minutes. Remove the spice purse and season with the cinnamon, nutmeg, and licorice root.

Puree the soup in a blender, being careful not to overload the blender with the hot soup. (Before turning on the machine, be sure the lid is tightly secured and covered with a towel to prevent the hot mixture from escaping.)

Strain through a fine strainer and serve with Spiced Crème Fraîche.

SPICED CRÈME FRAÎCHE

1 cup crème fraîche (page 221)

1/4 teaspoon salt

1/4 teaspoon freshly ground black pepper

1/4 teaspoon freshly grated nutmeg

1/4 teaspoon ground ginger

Whisk all ingredients together until smooth.

BROCCOLI SOUP

SERVES 6

Broccoli is in the family of cruciferous vegetables, the cancer-fighting powerhouses we all need more of in our diets. Eating a bowl of this silky, bright green soup is much more fun than a plate of steamed broccoli. If you are craving the childhood flavors of cheesy broccoli, garnish your soup with finely grated Cheddar or make some cheese toast for dipping.

1^1/$_2$ cups vegetable stock (page 220)

2 teaspoons fine sea salt

1 pound broccoli florets

^{1}/$_4$ cup unsalted butter

^{1}/$_2$ teaspoon ground white pepper

In a medium saucepan, bring the stock to a boil over high heat. Season with the salt, then drop in the broccoli florets and cook until they are soft and bright green, about 3 minutes. Immediately transfer the stock and broccoli to a blender along with the butter and white pepper. Before turning on the machine, be sure the lid is tightly secured and covered with a towel to prevent the hot mixture from escaping. Carefully blend the hot soup until it is nice and smooth.

Serve the soup immediately. If you are not serving it right away, you will need to chill the soup rapidly in a bowl set in a bowl of ice to preserve the green color.

TURNIP AND LEEK SOUP

SERVES 4 TO 6

This is our Southern twist on vichysoisse, the classic French potato-leek soup. And it's low carb to boot! Turnips lend a subtle spice to the soup without the sacrificing the rich creaminess. Be picky when choosing your turnips: make sure they are firm, not spongy, with a tinge of pink at the base of the stems.

1/4 cup unsalted butter

1 leek, white and light green parts, washed well, thinly sliced

1 teaspoon chopped garlic

1 bay leaf

Sprig of thyme

3 medium turnips, peeled and diced

1/4 cup white wine

3 cups vegetable stock (page 220)

1/4 cup heavy cream

1/4 teaspoon ground white pepper

1 teaspoon sugar

1 tablespoon fine sea salt

1 tablespoon crème fraîche (page 221)

In a large saucepan, melt the butter over medium heat. Add the leek, garlic, bay leaf, and thyme and cook until the sliced leek is softened, about 1 minute. Add the turnips and white wine and cook until the white wine has reduced by half, about 5 minutes. Add the stock, cream, white pepper, sugar, and salt and simmer until the turnips are very soft, at least 5 more minutes. Remove the bay leaf and thyme and transfer the soup to a blender along with the crème fraîche. Before turning on the machine, be sure the lid is tightly secured and covered with a towel to prevent the hot mixture from escaping. Blend the soup, until nice and smooth.

Serve immediately.

CREAMY PARSNIP SOUP

SERVES 6

When you want your kids to try new vegetables, the fragrant parsnip is a perfect one to start with. It's unobstrusive white color and intense natural sweetness will lure them back for another sip. If you are catering to a more adult palate, finish the soup with a drizzle of truffle oil for an elegant starter.

2 tablespoons light olive oil

2 pounds parsnips, peeled and thinly sliced

2 shallots, thinly sliced

4 cloves garlic, thinly sliced

1 fresh bay leaf

Sprig of thyme

2 teaspoons fine sea salt

1 teaspoon sugar

1/4 teaspoon ground white pepper

12 cups vegetable stock (page 220)

1 tablespoon crème fraîche (page 221)

In a large saucepan over medium heat, heat the oil. Add the parsnips, shallots, garlic, bay leaf, thyme, salt, sugar, and white pepper. Cook the vegetables until the shallots are soft, stirring frequently, about 5 minutes (be careful not to get much color on the parsnips). Add the stock and cook, simmering, for 30 minutes. Remove the bay leaf and thyme. Puree the soup in a blender, in batches. Before turning on the machine, be sure the lid is tightly secured and covered with a towel to prevent the hot mixture from escaping.

Once the soup is blended, stir in the crème fraîche and serve right away.

TOMATO SOUP

SERVES 6

When the tomatoes lined up on your counter in the summer start to get too soft to slice, it's time to make tomato soup. Use any variety or color of tomato that you have, as long as they are ripe and flavorful. While it is great served hot, this soup can also be served chilled, drizzled with yogurt, on a sultry summer day. Stash a pint of soup in the freezer for when it starts to get chilly and you need a partner for a grilled cheese sandwich.

1/4 cup extra-virgin olive oil

1 onion, thinly sliced

10 cloves garlic, smashed

1/2 teaspoon red pepper flakes

Sprig of rosemary

1 fresh bay leaf

2 1/2 pounds tomatoes, quartered

1 tablespoon fine sea salt

1 teaspoon sugar

1/4 teaspoon freshly ground black pepper

1 cup white wine

6 cups vegetable stock (page 220)

In a large saucepan, heat the oil over medium heat. Add the onion, garlic, red pepper flakes, rosemary, and bay leaf and cook for 3 minutes. Add the tomatoes, salt, sugar, and pepper and cook until the tomatoes start to break down, an additional 3 minutes. Add the white wine, bring the mixture to a simmer, and cook for 2 minutes. Add the stock, bring back to a simmer, decrease the heat to low, and cook for 30 minutes.

Remove the herbs and puree the soup in a blender, in batches, until smooth. Before turning on the machine, be sure the lid is tightly secured and covered with a towel to prevent the hot mixture from escaping.

Serve immediately.

BLACK-EYED PEA AND BARLEY BROTH

SERVES 4

This vegan soup will entice even a meat lover with its richness of flavor. Creamy black-eyed peas and toothsome barley add substance to the umami broth of mushroom and soy. Button mushrooms or creminis are a fine substitute if shiitakes are hard to find.

1/2 cup (4 ounces) black-eyed peas, soaked overnight

1/2 cup barley

2 tablespoons olive oil

1 cup shiitake mushroom caps, sliced 1/4 inch thick

1/4 cup finely diced carrots

1/4 cup finely diced shallots

1/4 cup finely diced celery

6 cups mushroom stock (page 220)

1/4 cup soy sauce

2 teaspoons sea salt

2 teaspoons coarsely ground black pepper

1 cup thinly sliced green onions, white and green
     parts, for garnish

In a small saucepan over high heat, bring 4 cups of water to a boil. Add the black-eyed peas and bring to a simmer. Cook, skimming off the scum that forms on the surface as needed, until tender, about 30 minutes. Strain the peas and reserve.

In a small saucepan over high heat, bring 4 cups of water to a boil. Add the barley and bring to a simmer. Cook the barley until tender, about 20 minutes. Strain the cooked barley in a colander under cold water and rinse well. Reserve until needed.

In a large saucepan over high heat, heat the olive oil to the smoking point. Add the sliced mushrooms and cook, stirring frequently, until they are nicely brown and fragrant, about 1 minute. Add the carrots, shallots, and celery and sauté for another minute. Add the stock, soy sauce, salt, pepper, peas, and barley and cook over a slow simmer to let the flavors develop, about 10 minutes.

Finish the soup with the sliced green onions and serve.

VEGETABLES

VEGETABLES

GENERATIONS ON BOTH SIDES of my family made their living by farming in central Mississippi and Louisiana. Some owned their land and others were sharecroppers. Cotton and soybeans were their money crops, and family gardens of vegetables and chickens fed the immediate family, kin, and close friends.

I grew up in West Monroe, but spent a lot of time in Winnsboro, the rural North Louisiana town where my father was from, and where my papaw Jack still had some land planted with corn. We often drove down a dusty road out to the "old place" where the small board-and-batten shack my dad grew up in still stood, mostly filled with corn husks.

The land on the other side of the road from the shack was mostly pine woods, but a clearing up front held troughs also full of corn. My papaw Jack, in his summertime straw cowboy hat, would yell out "come on UP" into the woods, and a herd of wild horses would come running. We were ready with pockets filled with sugar cubes that they would nuzzle out of the palms of our hands. My papaw named one pretty red-and-white painter horse Allison, after me.

Whenever I return to Winnsboro these days, I drive slowly along the highway with my windows down. The road is surrounded by soybean, cotton, and corn farms, which are dotted with rusted tractors and cotton gins, and not any different than when I was a kid. This feeling of knowing who I am and where I am from always comes over me on that highway and calms me. It also makes me understand why the dream of having my own garden (or farm) is never far away.

CREAMED COLLARDS

SERVES 4

Growing up in Mississippi, we Rushings always had a vegetable garden. After the tomatoes and eggplants were done for the season, my dad would plant green onions and greens for the fall, which would last until the first frost. This recipe is perfect for that last batch of greens, when the cool weather beckons the richness of nutmeg and cream.

2 bunches collard greens, thoroughly washed

3 tablespoons unsalted butter

3 shallots, finely minced

3 cloves garlic, peeled and smashed with the back
of a knife

Sprig of thyme

1 bay leaf

1 cup heavy cream

1/2 teaspoon freshly grated nutmeg

Salt and freshly ground black pepper

Fill a large stockpot with water and season it with enough salt so it tastes like sea water. Bring the water to a boil over high heat. Fill a bowl with ice water and have nearby.

Meanwhile, trim off the leaves of the collards, removing the central rib and stem; discard the ribs and stems. Drop the leaves into the rapidly boiling water and cook in batches, being careful not to drop the temperature of the water. Boil, uncovered, until the collards are tender, about 3 minutes. Transfer the cooked collards to the ice water bath to stop cooking and cool down.

Once the collards are cool, remove them from the ice water bath and squeeze them to remove as much water as you can. Chop the collards finely and reserve.

In a large sauté pan, melt the butter over medium heat. Decrease the heat to low and add the shallots, garlic, thyme, and bay leaf. Cook the shallots until they are soft and translucent, about 3 minutes. Add the cream, increase the heat to medium and cook until reduced by half, about 5 minutes. Remove the thyme and bay leaf. Stir in the collards and cook until they are warm and coated well with the cream.

To serve, sprinkle with freshly grated nutmeg and adjust the seasoning with salt and pepper, if needed.

FRICASSEE OF PEAS AND BEANS

SERVES 4

The summer market here in New Orleans always has a plethora of fresh peas: purple hull, pink-eyed, black-eyed, and crowders, perfect for combining in a simple stew or fricassee. It takes me back to Fourth of July at my Aunt Ruby's, when I was a young girl and we kids would be put to work shelling peas on the front steps. Little did I know then those skills would come in handy as a cook in Alain Ducasse's kitchen, where I was frequently delegated to an enormous mountain of peas for shelling duty.

8 ounces fresh black-eyed peas (or any other variety)

8 ounces fresh baby lima beans

1 bay leaf

4 sprigs thyme

6 cups chicken stock (page 220)

2 carrots, 1 trimmed and left whole and 1 finely diced

3 stalks celery, 1 trimmed and left whole and 2 finely diced

2 small onions, 1 halved and 1 finely diced

1 head garlic, top trimmed

1 teaspoon salt

1/2 teaspoon freshly ground black pepper

1/2 cup unsalted butter, diced

In a large saucepan, combine the peas, lima beans, bay leaf, 2 sprigs of the thyme, stock, whole carrot, whole celery stalk, onion halves, and garlic head. Place the saucepan over medium heat and bring to a simmer. (Do not season your beans now; you never season beans at the beginning of cooking because this would make them tough.)

While the beans are simmering, with a ladle or large spoon, skim off the scum on the surface. Cook the peas and beans until just tender, about 20 minutes. Once the beans are cooked, remove the herbs, carrot, celery, onion, and garlic from the pan and discard.

To finish the dish, add the diced carrot, diced celery, diced onion, salt, pepper, and butter to the pan. Return the stock with the beans and peas to a simmer over medium heat and cook until the liquid is glossy and emulsified, about 20 minutes.

Remove the leaves from the remaining 2 sprigs thyme. Garnish with the thyme leaves for fragrance and serve.

SWEET POTATO–TRUFFLE GRATIN

SERVES 12

We don't have much of a winter down here in Louisiana, which makes me miss my favorite holiday memories of New York City—the bright white just-fallen snow, the streets lined with Christmas lights, and the intoxicating smell of the fist-size winter black truffles in my garde manger cooler at Ducasse. Slade and I can't afford truffles like the ones I got to handle there, so instead we use truffle puree and truffle oil in this recipe, which are available year round and a fraction of the cost of fresh truffles.

1 1/4 teaspoons fine sea salt

1 teaspoon finely ground black pepper

1 tablespoon fresh thyme leaves,

1 tablespoon chopped garlic

2 tablespoon white truffle oil (see Sources, page 223)

1 (7/8-ounce) tube black truffle puree (see Sources, page 223)

1 cup freshly grated Parmesan cheese

6 cups heavy cream

3 large sweet potatoes

6 large Yukon gold potatoes

2 tablespoons unsalted butter

Preheat the oven to 350°F.

To make the truffle cream, in a saucepan, combine the salt, pepper, thyme, garlic, truffle oil, truffle puree, Parmesan, and cream. Bring the mixture to a simmer over high heat, whisking occasionally. Once the mixture reaches a simmer, turn off the heat and let cool to room temperature.

Meanwhile, have a bowl of cool water nearby. Peel all of the potatoes, submerging them in the cool water to prevent discoloration. With 1 tablespoon of the butter, grease the bottom and sides of a 9 by 13-inch casserole dish. Using a mandoline, carefully slice the potatoes 1/8 inch thick, keeping the sweet potato slices and Yukon gold potato slices separate.

Starting with the Yukon golds, arrange the potato slices in a shingle-like pattern in the casserole dish, overlapping the edges slightly. Using a 1/2-cup measure, scoop and pour the truffle cream evenly over the layer of potatoes, making sure to mix the cream each time before scooping it.

Next, arrange a layer of sweet potatoes and cream. Repeat the process, alternating layers of Yukon golds and sweet potatoes, until you have nine layers, ending with the Yukon golds. Dot the top of the gratin with the remaining 1 tablespoon of butter. Lay a sheet of parchment or waxed paper over the top.

Cover the casserole tightly with aluminum foil, place on a baking sheet, and bake for 1 3/4 hours. Remove the foil and parchment paper and bake until the top is browned, about 15 more minutes.

Let the gratin rest for at least 30 minutes before cutting and serving.

YELLOW SQUASH MARMALADE

No it's not squash preserves, but the chunky texture and richness bring to mind a kind of marmalade. Cooked yellow squash tends to get watery, but removing the seeds eliminates that distraction. Dicing the squash is all the work you have to do; the butter and onions do the rest. Serve this with a piece of grilled fish and a tomato and basil salad.

6 medium yellow squash

1 medium white onion

1/2 cup unsalted butter

4 cloves garlic, smashed

2 sprigs thyme

1 fresh bay leaf

Fine sea salt and coarsely ground black pepper

Using a vegetable peeler, peel the squash. Quarter the squash lengthwise, remove the seeds, and cut the squash into 1/4-inch dice. Cut the onion into 1/4-inch dice as well.

Melt the butter in a large sauté pan over medium heat. Add the onion, garlic, thyme, and bay leaf and cook until the onions are translucent, about 3 minutes. Add the diced squash, season with the salt and pepper, and cook until the squash is tender, about 5 minutes. Remove the bay leaf and thyme before serving.

ROASTED OKRA WITH CHILI OIL

SERVES 4

Okra is a beloved vegetable to some, but its slimy texture in soups and stews is not for everyone's palate. At the restaurant, we like to roast it whole alongside lamb in the rendered fat until it is crispy. Drizzling it with olive oil and roasting it in the oven yields an equally crispy, non-slimy result.

1 pound okra

1/2 teaspoon salt

1/4 teaspoon freshly ground black pepper

1/4 cup chili oil (page 222)

Preheat the oven to 400°F. Toss together the okra, salt, pepper, and chili oil in a bowl. Spread out evenly on a baking sheet and roast in the oven until evenly browned, about 15 minutes.

Serve hot and crispy.

BUTTER-GLAZED GREEN CABBAGE

SERVES 4

Slade and I both grew up eating cabbage cooked soul-food fashion—stewed all day with lots of onion, ham hock, and water. A bowl of this soupy soft cabbage with cornbread for sopping was a meal in itself. Instead of cooking ours all day, we blanch the individual leaves quickly and glaze them in a silky butter sauce. There is something magical about this simple combination of earthy cabbage, sweet butter, and salt. It shines as a side dish for chicken or pork chops and is a must with black-eyed peas for New Year's Day.

1 head green cabbage

1 cup unsalted butter, cut in 1/2-inch cubes

2 tablespoons chopped fresh chives

In a large saucepot, bring 4 quarts water with 2 tablespoons salt to a boil over high heat.

Fill a bowl with ice water and have nearby. Core and quarter the cabbage head. Separate the individual layers and discard any bruised outer leaves. Once the water reaches a boil, submerge all of the cabbage leaves in the water, stirring occasionally to ensure even cooking. Blanch the leaves until tender to the tooth, but still slightly firm, 3 to 4 minutes.

Transfer all the leaves to the ice water bath to cool. Reserve 1/2 cup of the cabbage blanching water and discard the rest. Once the cabbage is cool, remove from the ice bath and dry thoroughly in between layers of paper towels.

Place a large sauté pan over medium-low heat and add the reserved cabbage blanching liquid to the pan. Carefully whisk in the butter, piece by piece, until a creamy butter sauce is formed. Add the cabbage to the pan and rewarm, coating completely with sauce.

Sprinkle the cabbage with the chives and serve.

CELERY ROOT PUREE

MAKES 4 CUPS

Celery root, or celeriac, is a lovely celery-scented root vegetable. Traditionally prepared cold in a creamy rémoulade sauce, it also makes a surprisingly versatile hot dish. It is a great, low-carb replacement for mashed potatoes that goes well with seafood, chicken, or pork. You can also thin out this puree with vegetable stock for a silky soup and garnish it with a spicy mustard oil.

2 celery roots, peeled and cut into 1-inch dice

8 cloves garlic

4 cups whole milk

1/4 cup unsalted butter

1 teaspoon salt

1/4 teaspoon ground white pepper

Combine the celery root, garlic, and milk in a saucepan and bring to a simmer over medium heat. Cook until the celery root can be mashed easily between two fingers, about 25 minutes. Drain through a sieve, reserving 1 cup of the hot milk.

Combine the cooked celery root and garlic in a blender with the reseved milk, butter, salt, and white pepper and puree until silky smooth. Before turning on the machine, be sure the lid is tightly secured and covered with a towel to prevent the hot mixture from escaping.

Serve right away.

OYSTER–SWISS CHARD GRATIN WITH COUNTRY BACON

SERVES 8

Swiss chard is a winter green that is in season just as oysters are at their peak. As the weather cools, the chard gets sweeter and the oysters get saltier, achieving a beautiful balance of earth and sea when together in the same bite. We use big, sweet Louisiana oysters, but any oyster will do.

3 thick slices smoky bacon, cut into small dice

2 tablespoons unsalted butter

1 small onion, minced

2 cloves garlic, minced

2 bunches Swiss chard, stemmed, leaves chopped into 1/2-inch dice

2 cups heavy cream

1/8 teaspoon freshly grated nutmeg

18 oysters, freshly shucked, patted dry, and coarsely chopped

1/2 teaspoon salt

1/2 teaspoon freshly ground black pepper

1 cup freshly grated Parmesan cheese

1 cup fresh bread crumbs

Preheat the oven to 400°F.

Brown the bacon in a large sauté pan over medium heat. Add the butter, onion, garlic, and Swiss chard and sauté until the chard is completely wilted. Remove from the heat. Pour the mixture into a colander set in the sink and squeeze out all excess liquid. Reserve.

Return the pan to the stove and add the cream and nutmeg. Bring to a boil over high heat, then decrease the heat to medium-low so the cream does not boil over. Cook the cream until it reduces to 1 cup. Set aside to cool.

In a bowl, combine the chard mixture, cooled cream, and oysters. Mix well and season with salt and pepper. Spoon the mixture into a 3-quart gratin dish. Using the back of a spoon, spread the mixture evenly. In a small bowl, mix together the Parmesan cheese and bread crumbs and sprinkle the topping evenly over the gratin.

Bake until the mixture is bubbling around the sides and the crust is lightly golden brown, about 12 minutes.

Remove from the oven and let cool slightly before serving.

SAUTÉ-STEAMED BABY BOK CHOY

Serves 4

Sauté-steaming is a technique I learned in the kitchen of Ducasse, as the majority of my time there was spent cleaning and cooking vegetables. What I love about this technique is how fast it steams the vegetables after you add the water to the hot pan, and how it also adds a touch of flavor with the oil and garlic that you would not get with basic steaming. Feel free to substitute just about anything—broccoli, cauliflower, squash, turnips, carrots, or sweet potatoes. You can cook almost any vegetable this way, except for something with a thick fibrous skin, such as green beans. To ensure fast, even cooking, don't overcrowd the pan.

4 heads baby bok choy

1 tablespoon extra-virgin olive oil

6 cloves garlic, crushed

1/2 teaspoon salt

1/4 teaspoon freshly ground black pepper

2 tablespoons water

Trim off the outside leaves of the bok choy and any discolored parts on the bottom stem. Halve the bok choy and soak the halves in cold water for 5 minutes to remove any dirt. Transfer the bok choy to paper towels to dry.

Heat a large sauté pan with a tight-fitting lid over high heat. Once it is hot, add the oil and the garlic and sauté the garlic for 30 seconds, letting it brown slightly and become fragrant. Add the bok choy and season with the salt and pepper. Add the 2 tablespoons water and quickly cover with the lid, decrease the heat to low, and steam for 1 minute.

Remove from the heat and serve immediately.

TURNIPS, BOULANGERIE STYLE

SERVES 6

The boulangerie style of cooking potatoes was classically done in a large oven under roasting chickens so the drippings from the birds fell on the potatoes, giving them a rich, caramelized coating. We love to roast sweet and earthy turnips in chicken fat when we are roasting a chicken at home. This presentation is a bit more elegant, all layered and glazed but with the same complementary flavors, and looks lovely on the table. If you want to omit the bacon and have olive oil (or even better, chicken fat in the fridge) to cook the shallots, please by all means substitute.

3 ounces sliced bacon, finely chopped

6 medium shallots, finely minced

8 garlic cloves, thinly sliced

1 1/2 teaspoons fresh thyme leaves

5 turnips, peeled

2 russet potatoes, peeled

3 tablespoons unsalted butter, diced

1 teaspoon fine sea salt

1/2 teaspoon finely ground black pepper

1 3/4 cups chicken stock (page 220)

Preheat the oven to 350°F. Butter a 9 by 13-inch ovenproof casserole dish.

In a sauté pan over medium heat, cook the bacon for 3 minutes to start rendering the fat. Add the shallots, garlic, and 1 teaspoon of the thyme leaves. Cook until the shallots are soft and translucent, about 5 minutes. Remove the mixture from the heat and reserve.

Using a mandoline, slice the turnips and potatoes on the thinnest setting, about 1/16 inch thick. Arrange an overlapping layer of turnips and potatoes, alternating them side by side, in the casserole dish and spread one-third of the shallot and bacon mixture evenly on top. Season with some of the salt and pepper and dot with one-quarter of the diced butter. Repeat this process three more times to make four layers total. Dot the top layer with the remaining butter, season with salt and pepper, and top with the remaining 1/2 teaspoon thyme leaves. Add the stock to the dish, pouring it in around the edges.

Cover the casserole tightly with aluminum foil and bake for 1 1/2 hours. Remove the foil and cook for 20 more minutes to caramelize the top layer.

Let it rest for 30 minutes, then cut into portions and serve.

PASTA AND GRAINS

PASTA AND GRAINS

I AM SURE THE THOUGHT of spending all day in the kitchen elbow deep in flour making dough drives some people absolutely mad. Luckily, from the time I started cooking I was able to find that making things with my hands produced a meditative-like comfort, where the process is just as important as the finished result.

One of the most inspiring examples of this that I have ever seen was on a trip to San Francisco that coincided with the Tibetan New Year. Buddhist monks were displaying their elaborate sculptures made of colored butter, a tradition dating back to the early seventeenth century. They had been working on them for months. The sculptures were truly breathtaking and, in the Buddhist tradition, impermanent. At the end of the celebration, all of the butter sculptures were melted. That is where I find myself when I spend the day making pasta. That doesn't mean Slade and I don't buy a box of dried pasta off the shelf—we do. But when I have the luxury of spending the day with the tradition of forming noodles made of the most basic of ingredients, I cherish it. Of course, those homemade noodles are impermanent, too, providing full, comforted tummies just for the dinner hour. What's more important is the long, lovely day I spent getting there.

SWEET POTATO PAPPARDELLE WITH RICH SHIITAKE SAUCE

SERVES 6

This pasta utilizes two locally abundant ingredients: sweet potatoes and shiitake mushrooms. A vegetarian dish, it is deceptively rich. The beautiful orange ribbons of pasta are glazed in a simple sauce of mushroom stock and butter and finished off with some shavings of sheep cheese—gilding the lily, so to speak.

Sweet Potato Pasta

2 cups sweet potato juice (peel 10 sweet potatoes and push through a vegetable juicer), carrot juice is a good substitute
2 cups durum flour
1 teaspoon salt
1 teaspoon extra-virgin olive oil
1 egg

Rich Shiitake Sauce

1 pound fresh shiitake mushrooms
1/4 cup extra-virgin olive oil
1 cup unsalted butter, cut into small cubes
Garlic confit (page 221)
2 cups mushroom stock (page 220)
Salt and freshly ground black pepper

4 ounces sheep cheese (such as Thomasville Tomme), shaved, for garnish
Fresh herbs (such as chervil sprigs or chives), for garnish

To make the pasta, in a large saucepan, cook the sweet potato juice over medium heat until it is reduced by three-quarters and thick, with the consistency of paint. Let the reduction cool.

In a stand mixer fitted with the dough hook attachment, mix the flour and salt. Add the sweet potato reduction and mix well at medium speed. Add the olive oil and egg and mix until the dough comes together in a ball. Continue to work the dough in the mixer for 5 minutes. Remove the dough from the mixer and shape it into a ball. Wrap the dough in plastic wrap and place in the refrigerator for at least 1 hour to rest.

Set up your pasta machine. Lightly flour a baking sheet and have nearby. Halve the dough, keep half covered in plastic. Lightly flour your work surface.

Roll half of the dough through your pasta machine from the largest setting through each progressively smaller setting, stopping at the second smallest setting.

Using a pizza cutter or knife, cut your dough into long, 1-inch-wide ribbons. Place the cut pasta on the prepared baking sheet and repeat the rolling and cutting process with the other half of the dough. Let the pasta ribbons rest uncovered while the sauce cooks.

To make the sauce, remove the stems from the shiitake mushrooms and reserve them for stock or other use. Cut the mushroom caps into wedges and reserve.

Bring a large pot of well-salted water to a boil.

Heat a large sauté pan over medium-high heat until smoking, then decrease the heat slightly. Add the oil to the pan, then the shiitake mushroom caps (do not season with salt just yet), and caramelize them lightly for 1 minute. Decrease the heat to low and add the butter to the pan. Once the butter is foaming and brown, add the confit and stock, season with salt to taste, and bring to a simmer. Once a light sauce begins to form in the pan, whisk all the elements together until they are emulsified. Remove the pan from the heat while you cook the pasta.

To finish the pasta, drop the pasta ribbons into the rapidly boiling water and cook for 30 seconds. Drain the pasta through a colander and return it to the pasta cooking pot. Add the mushroom sauce to the pasta and, using tongs, coat the pasta well in the sauce.

Adjust the seasoning, then divide the pasta among six dishes. Top with a few shavings of sheep cheese and fresh herbs.

FREGOLA WITH COLLARD GREENS AND LEMON

SERVES 4

Down here, the go-to recipe for collard greens involves a big pot, a ham hock, and an hour of cooking. A more modern approach results in additional nutrition combined with a shorter cooking time. In this dish, we thinly slice and quickly steam collards so they stay bright green, then we add nutty fregola (a small, round semolina pasta), toasted garlic, and a bright lemon broth. The result is like a chic city makeover of these country greens.

1/2 cup dried fregola pasta

1 bunch collard greens, well washed

1 lemon

2 tablespoons extra-virgin olive oil

4 large cloves garlic, thinly sliced

1/2 cup water

15 grape tomatoes, halved

1 teaspoon salt

1/2 teaspoon freshly ground black pepper

To cook the pasta, bring 4 cups of water and 1 teaspoon of salt to a boil in a medium sauce-pan over high heat. Add the fregola and cook until al dente, about 8 minutes. Drain in a colander and rinse under cold water. Set aside.

To prepare the greens, trim the tough stems from the collard greens and discard them. Cut the leaves into thin strips and reserve in a bowl.

To prepare the lemon, using a vegetable peeler, first peel off thin strips of yellow zest from the lemon and cut the strips into matchsticks (julienne). Slice off both ends of the lemon and then trim away all remaining peel and white pith. Holding the lemon in one hand, use a sharp knife to cut away and free each lemon segment. Reserve the segments and julienned zest in a bowl, and discard the rest of the lemon.

To make the sauce, heat a large sauté pan with a tight-fitting lid over medium-high heat. Add the olive oil and garlic and carefully toast the garlic slices until they are light brown, about 1 minute. Carefully add the collard greens and water and immediately cover with the lid. Cook, covered, for 2 minutes. Uncover, and add the lemon zest and lemon segments, tomatoes, cooked fregola, salt, and pepper. Cook uncovered for another 2 minutes, stirring to combine all of the ingredients.

Serve immediately.

BUTTERMILK AND CHIVE SPAETZLE

SERVES 4

To Southerners, a simple boiled dough is a dumpling. Spaetzle is a small German dumpling that elegantly cradles a rich sauce, such as a braise. We like to serve them with rustic meats, such as veal cheeks or braised chicken thighs. If you crave a bit of green, sauté the spaetzle with sweet peas or bitter broccoli rabe.

2 cups all-purpose flour

1 1/2 teaspoons salt

1/2 teaspoon freshly grated nutmeg

1/2 teaspoon freshly ground black pepper

4 large eggs

3/4 cup buttermilk

Fresh chives, chopped

Unsalted butter, for sautéing the spaetzle

Bring a large pot of salted water to a boil over high heat. Fill a bowl with ice water and have nearby.

To make the spaetzle dough, whisk together the flour, salt, nutmeg, and pepper in a large bowl. In a separate bowl, whisk together the eggs and buttermilk. Make a well in the center of the dry ingredients and pour the wet ingredients into the well. Using a whisk, bring together the wet and dry ingredients, working from the inside out to ensure there are no lumps. Lastly, fold the chives into the dough and mix well.

To cook the spaetzle, once the water has come to a boil, put all of the dough into a metal colander with large holes and rest the colander on rim of the pot of boiling water. Using a spatula, press the dough through the holes in the colander into the boiling water. Let the spaetzle cook until all of the dumplings float to the surface, about 3 minutes. Transfer them with a slotted spoon to the ice bath to cool down.

To serve, sauté the spaetzle in a hot pan with butter until they are crispy.

SHRIMP RAVIOLI IN ANDOUILLE BROTH

SERVES 4

The use of store-bought wonton skins in this recipe make this one-pot ravioli dish a cinch to prepare. Poaching the ravioli directly in the broth not only saves time, but more importantly, allows the flavor to fully permeate the dough. Another plus: the depth of flavor of the andouille and soy broth will beguile your audience into thinking you spent all day in the kitchen.

BROTH

1/4 cup soy sauce

12 cups water

3 pounds andouille sausage, sliced 1/8 inch thick

FILLING

1/2 pound shrimp, peeled and deveined

1/2 teaspoon ground white pepper

1 teaspoon fine sea salt

1 teaspoon chopped fresh ginger

1 teaspoon toasted sesame oil

1/4 cup loosely packed cilantro leaves, chopped

2 bunches green onions (about 14 stems), white and
    green parts, thinly sliced

1 (12-ounce) package wonton wrappers

1 pound shiitake mushrooms, stems removed and
    reserved for another use, caps sliced

2 carrots, peeled and julienned

To make the broth, in a large saucepan, combine the soy sauce, water, and andouille. Bring to a boil over high heat. Once it comes to a boil, immediately decrease the heat to a slow simmer and simmer the broth for about 30 minutes.

Meanwhile, prepare the filling. Chop the shrimp finely and place in a small bowl. Add the white pepper, salt, ginger, sesame oil, cilantro, and half the green onions and mix all together until well combined. Using a tablespoon measure, scoop out sixteen equal portions of filling. Roll the filling between your palms to form marble-size balls and place them on a plate. You can wet your palms with water periodically to keep the filling from sticking to your hands.

Remove the ravioli skins from the wrapper and place them on your work surface. Cover them with a slightly damp towel so they don't dry out. Have a small cup of cool water nearby to use to seal the ravioli.

To assemble the ravioli, place one wonton wrapper in the palm of your hand and place a ball of filling in the center. Dip one finger in the water and wet all edges of the wonton skin around the filling. Cover with a second wonton wrapper, cupping the ravioli in the palm of your hand, and pinch the edges of the ravioli closed with your thumb and index finger. (See photos on pages 128–29.) Place the ravioli on another plate and continue until all the ravioli are assembled.

To cook the ravioli, return the andouille broth to a boil and then immediately drop the ravioli into the broth, one by one. Add the mushrooms and carrots and return the broth to a simmer. Cook for 3 minutes, stirring occasionally to keep the ravioli from sticking together.

To serve, divide the ravioli among four bowls and top with the broth, sliced andouille, and the vegetables. Garnish the dish with the remaining green onions.

SEASHELL PASTA WITH CRAB AND HERBS

Serves 6

Probably the most annoying part of cooking pasta is that you need an extra pot of water to boil the pasta. This recipe cooks the pasta as you would risotto—in one pan, adding hot liquid to it little by little. The result is not only one less pot to clean, but the addition of water combines with the starch of the pasta and the butter, coating the pasta in a lovely sauce. Kids love pasta this way, but if they are super finicky, leave the crab and herbs out of theirs.

3 tablespoons unsalted butter

1 leek, white and light green parts, washed and
   thinly sliced

1 teaspoon chopped garlic

1 bay leaf

2 sprigs thyme

1 pound dried seashell pasta

6 cups hot water

8 ounces fresh crabmeat, picked over to remove shells

1 1/2 teaspoons fine sea salt

1 teaspoon coarsely ground black pepper

2 teaspoons chopped fresh parsley

1 tablespoon chopped fresh chives

1/4 cup freshly grated good-quality Parmesan cheese

In a large straight-sided sauté pan, melt 1 tablespoon of the butter over medium heat. Add the leek, garlic, bay leaf, and thyme sprigs and cook until the leek begins to soften, about 1 minute. Add the pasta to the pan and 2 1/2 cups of the hot water. Cook, stirring frequently as you would risotto, until most of the liquid has been absorbed, 5 to 7 minutes. Add the remaining 2 1/2 cups of water and cook, stirring often, until the pasta is cooked and there is about 1/2 cup of liquid remaining in the pasta. Add the crab, remaining 2 tablespoons of butter, salt, pepper, parsley, chives, and Parmesan.

Stir well and cook until the butter is emulsified into a sauce and the crab is warmed through, about 3 minutes. Serve right away.

POTATO GNOCCHI WITH MUSTARD-GREEN PESTO

SERVES 4

Gnocchi are Italian potato dumplings that are like a sophisticated comfort food. When done properly, they are a perfect balance of softness and structure. And they are delicious coated in a sharp, garlicky sauce like pesto. Italians often substitute peppery arugula for the traditional basil in pesto. Our Southern version uses peppery mustard greens instead.

1 cup tightly packed mustard greens, washed and stemmed

3 tablespoons pine nuts, toasted

2 tablespoons freshly grated Parmesan cheese

1 teaspoon minced garlic

1/2 cup extra-virgin olive oil

3/4 teaspoon fine sea salt

10 ounces russet potatoes (about 2 large)

1/2 cup all-purpose flour

1 large egg yolk

1/8 teaspoon ground black pepper

Shaved Parmesan cheese, for garnish

To make the pesto, combine the mustard greens, pine nuts, Parmesan cheese, garlic, olive oil, and 1/4 teaspoon of the salt in a blender and blend on high speed until smooth, about 2 minutes; reserve.

To prepare the gnocchi, preheat the oven to 400°F. Bake the potatoes until soft to the touch, about 30 minutes.

Bring a large pot of salted water to a boil over high heat. Once it reaches a boil, decrease the heat to a strong simmer.

While the potatoes are still hot, using a kitchen towel, hold the potato in one hand while with the other you peel away the skin with a knife; discard the skin. Push the flesh of the potato through a potato ricer (if you don't have a ricer, you can press the warm potatoes through a flour sifter) into a large bowl.

To make the dough, while the riced potato is still warm, add the flour, egg yolk, the remaining 1/2 teaspoon salt, and pepper. Using your fingertips, stir everything together. Turn the dough out onto a floured surface and knead 3 or 4 times. Dust the palms of your hands with flour and cut the dough into thirds. Quickly working with the dough while it is still warm, roll each third into a rope about 1/2 inch in diameter. Cut the ropes into 1-inch pieces. (See photos on pages 134–35.)

Lightly dust a baking sheet with flour, and also flour a dinner fork. To form each gnocchi, using your thumb, roll each piece along the back of the tines of the fork to make indentations and gently roll the dough off the fork. Place the formed gnocchi on the prepared baking sheet. Repeat until all the gnocchi are formed.

Slip the gnocchi into the simmering water and cook until they all float to the top, about 2 minutes. Transfer the floating gnocchi with a slotted spoon to a bowl and toss with the pesto.

Serve garnished with shaved Parmesan.

SWEET POTATO GNOCCHI WITH PECANS AND BROWN BUTTER

Serves 4

Admittedly, we will try to incorporate sweet potato into just about any recipe. It is such a versatile vegetable, and one of the most healthy and inexpensive available. Even though they are potatoes, they do not have the starch content of russets, therefore you need both kinds for this recipe. The aroma of the brown butter and toasted pecans from this dish will mingle perfectly on a table with your other holiday sides.

3/4 cup kosher salt

3/4 pound russet potatoes (about 3)

1/2 pound sweet potato (about 1 large)

1 1/2 teaspoons fine sea salt

1 large egg yolk

3/4 cup all-purpose flour, plus more for dusting

1 1/2 tablespoons extra-virgin olive oil

3 tablespoons unsalted butter

1/2 cup pecan halves, chopped

Preheat the oven to 375°F. Spread the kosher salt on a baking sheet. Set all of the potatoes (russet and sweet potato) on the salt and bake until tender, about 1 hour. Let cool and discard the salt.

To make the dough, peel the baked potatoes. Work them through a potato ricer, or press through a flour sifter, into a large bowl. Mix in 1 teaspoon of the sea salt, the egg yolks, and the flour. Turn the dough onto a lightly floured work surface and knead it gently 3 or 4 times, adding more flour if necessary to keep the dough from sticking. Cut the dough into six equal pieces and cover with a clean, barely damp kitchen towel.

Bring a large pot of water to a boil over high heat. Fill a bowl with ice water and have ready.

Lightly flour a baking sheet and also flour a dinner fork. To form the gnocchi, working with one piece at a time, roll the gnocchi dough on a lightly floured work surface into a 3/4-inch-thick rope. Cut the rope into 1/2-inch pieces. To form each gnocchi, using your thumb, roll each piece along the back of the tines of the fork to make indentations, then gently roll the dough off the fork. Transfer the gnocchi to the prepared baking sheet. Repeat until all the gnocchi are formed.

To cook the gnocchi, salt the boiling water. Once it reaches a boil, decrease the heat to a strong simmer. Add half of the gnocchi and stir gently until they begin to rise to the surface, about 2 minutes. Using a slotted spoon, transfer the gnocchi to the ice water to cool down, then drain well on paper towels. Repeat with the remaining gnocchi.

To finish the dish, in a large bowl, toss the gnocchi with the olive oil, and spread them out on a large baking sheet.

In a very large skillet, melt 2 tablespoons of the butter. Cook the butter over moderate heat until it begins to brown, about 1 minute. Add one-third of the pecans and cook, stirring, until the nuts are toasted, about 2 minutes. Add half of the gnocchi and cook until they are golden brown and warmed through, about 2 minutes. Season with one-third of the remaining sea salt and transfer the gnocchi to a bowl. Repeat with the remaining butter, pecans, and gnocchi.

Serve immediately.

CREAMY COCONUT RICE

SERVES 4

Since we love cooking Asian food at home, we almost always have a large bag of Japanese or short-grain rice on hand. You can use Japanese rice in any recipe that calls for short-grain rice, for example, in place of Arborio rice in risotto. We cook this rice dish like risotto, starting with white wine and shallots and gradually adding liquid as it cooks. The coconut recalls Thai and Caribbean dishes, but we like to serve it with New Orleans flair, alongside spicy crawfish.

2 tablespoons olive oil

2 medium shallots, finely diced

4 cloves garlic, smashed

1 cup short-grain or Japanese rice

1/4 cup white wine

4 cups water

1 cup coconut puree (see Sources, page 223)

2 teaspoons salt

1 teaspoon freshly ground black pepper

Heat a medium saucepan over medium heat. Add the olive oil, shallots, and garlic and decrease the heat to medium-low. Cook until the shallots are soft and translucent, about 2 minutes. Add the rice and stir for about 1 minute. Add the white wine, stir to incorporate, and cook until the wine is almost fully absorbed. Add the water, 1/2 cup at a time, while stirring, making sure it is almost fully absorbed each time before adding the next portion. Once all of the water has been added and is completely absorbed, add the coconut puree and stir well.

Remove the garlic, season with salt and pepper, and serve.

"SHRIMP CREOLE" RISOTTO

SERVES 4

The classic shrimp creole is a rustic dish comprised of shrimp stewed in a spicy tomato sauce served over white rice. This highbrow version maintains all of the flavors of the original, but with separate, perfectly cooked ingredients. Risotto is the creamy vehicle that brings all of the flavors together in each bite.

24 medium shrimp (about 1 pound), peeled and
    deviened, shells reserved

2 cups cold water

5 tablespoons light olive oil

1 red bell pepper, cored, seeded, and minced

2 medium carrots, minced

2 stalks celery, minced

2 small white onions, minced

1-inch-wide strip orange zest, white pith removed

1 jalapeño chile, minced

2 bay leaves

4 cloves garlic

Sprig of flat-leaf parsley

2 sprigs thyme, plus 1 tablespoon thyme leaves,
    for garnish

3/4 teaspoon fine sea salt

3/4 teaspoon freshly ground black pepper

1 (12-ounce) can imported Italian whole tomatoes
    with juice

1 cup white wine

1 cup Arborio rice

4 cups chicken stock (page 220), warmed

1/4 cup unsalted butter

Zest and juice of 1 lemon

2 green onions, white and green parts, cut into thin
    rings, for garnish

To make the sauce, place all of the shrimp shells in a medium saucepan and cover with the cold water. Bring to a boil over high heat and then decrease to a simmer. Skim any impurities that rise to the surface off with a ladle and discard. Cook the stock for 25 minutes, then strain through a fine-mesh sieve and reserve.

In a large sauté pan, heat 1 tablespoon of the olive oil until smoking. Decrease the heat to medium and add the bell pepper, half of the carrot, half of the celery, half of the minced onion, the orange zest, chile, 1 bay leaf, 2 cloves of the garlic, sprig of parsley, 1 sprig of thyme, 1/4 teaspoon of the salt, and 1/4 teaspoon of the pepper. Cook the vegetables until tender, about 3 minutes.

Add the tomatoes and 1/2 cup of the white wine and cook for 3 minutes. Add enough of the shrimp stock to just cover the vegetables with liquid (about 1 cup). Cook the sauce for 20 minutes. Remove all the herbs and puree in a blender until smooth. (Before turning on the machine, be sure the lid is tightly secured and covered with a towel to prevent the hot mixture from escaping.)

Return the sauce to the pan on a warm stove and reserve.

To make the risotto, place a saucepan over medium-high heat. When hot, add 1 tablespoon of the olive oil. Add the remaining onions, carrots, celery, garlic cloves, thyme, bay leaf, 1/4 teaspoon salt, and 1/4 teaspoon pepper. Decrease the heat to medium and cook the vegetables until soft, about 3 minutes. Add the rice to the pan, stir, and cook for 1 minute more. Add the remaining 1/2 cup white wine and cook until most of the wine is absorbed in the rice. Add the warm chicken stock in 1/4-cup increments, stirring occasionally, until the liquid is absorbed. Continue adding chicken stock, stirring, until the rice is al dente.

Finish the risotto with the butter and lemon zest and juice. Remove the herbs and adjust the seasoning.

To prepare the shrimp, heat the remaining 3 tablespoons of the olive oil in a large sauté pan over high heat until smoking. Season the shrimp on both sides with the remaining 1/4 teaspoon salt and 1/4 teaspoon pepper. Decrease the heat to medium-high and add the shrimp. Cook the shrimp on each side for 1 minute, to give them nice color, then transfer them to a plate.

For each serving, divide the risotto evenly among four bowls and top each with six shrimp. Spoon the sauce around the risotto and garnish with green onions and fresh thyme leaves.

BLACK TRUFFLE GRITS

SERVES 6

This dish is really the ultimate in "high-low" cooking. The high-class truffle elevates the lowly grits into a dish reserved for your most special occasions. Black truffle puree is a good chunk of change, so serve this with an inexpensive, yet unctuous braised meat, such as beef short ribs or pig cheeks. If you can't find cuts such as those, try it with a simple chicken dish.

4 cups whole milk

1 cup quick grits

1/2 cup unsalted butter

1/4 cup heavy cream

1 1/2 teaspoons salt

1 teaspoon black pepper

1 (7/8-ounce) tube black truffle puree (see Sources, page 223)

2 teaspoons white truffle oil (see Sources, page 223)

To prepare the grits, warm the milk in a medium saucepan over medium heat until bubbles form around the edges, about 5 minutes. Whisk the grits into the milk and decrease the heat to medium-low. Let the grits cook for 10 minutes, whisking occasionally to prevent clumps. Finish the grits by whisking in the butter, heavy cream, salt, pepper, truffle puree, and truffle oil. Cover the pot of grits with a lid and remove from the heat.

Serve immediately or hold in a warm area, covered, for up to 20 minutes.

CORNMEAL POLENTA WITH GOAT CHEESE

SERVES 4

Polenta is made from cornmeal, but a larger grind than the cornmeal we use for making cornbread. We use the fine cornbread cornmeal instead, resulting in a much quicker cooking time than the hour or so it takes for traditional polenta. Tangy goat cheese makes this side dish scream out for game meat in a dark, fruity sauce.

3 cups whole milk

1/2 teaspoon salt

1/2 cup fine cornmeal

4 ounces Louisiana goat cheese (or any chèvre will do)

1 tablespoon unsalted butter

Bring the milk to a boil over high heat in a small saucepan. Add the salt and, using a whisk, whisk in the cornmeal. Decrease the heat to medium-high and cook the polenta until it starts to thicken, about 3 minutes. Decrease the heat to low and cook for about 10 minutes, stirring frequently to make sure nothing is sticking to the bottom of the pan. The polenta is ready when the cornmeal is no longer gritty. Add the goat cheese and butter, stirring to incorporate.

Serve immediately or hold in a warm area, covered, until needed.

PECAN RICE

This dish is a rice pilaf, where the rice is toasted in oil with onion before liquid is added to finish the cooking. The addition of chopped pecans adds an additional nuttiness to the toasted rice. Pilafs are usually made with a meat-based stock like chicken; if you want a vegetarian version, you can easily substitute vegetable stock or water. We like to serve this with the Coffee Roasted Pork Loin (page 184) or alongside our turkey at Thanksgiving.

1 tablespoon olive oil

1/4 cup chopped pecans

1 cup long-grain rice

2 tablespoons finely diced shallots

1 tablespoon finely diced carrot

1/4 teaspoon fine sea salt

1/8 teaspoon freshly ground black pepper

2 cups chicken stock (page 220)

1 tablespoon thinly sliced green onions, white and
    green parts

Place a saucepan with a tight-fitting lid over medium heat. Add the olive oil and heat for 1 minute. Add the pecans and toast, stirring with a wooden spoon, until the nuts are fragrant, about 1 minute. Add the rice and toast for 2 minutes, stirring frequently. Add the shallots, carrot, salt, and pepper.

Cook the rice and the vegetables for an additional 3 minutes. Add the stock, increase the heat to high, and bring the mixture to a simmer. Decrease the heat to low, cover, and cook for 12 minutes. Remove from the heat and let the rice sit, covered, for another 10 minutes.

Stir in the green onions before serving.

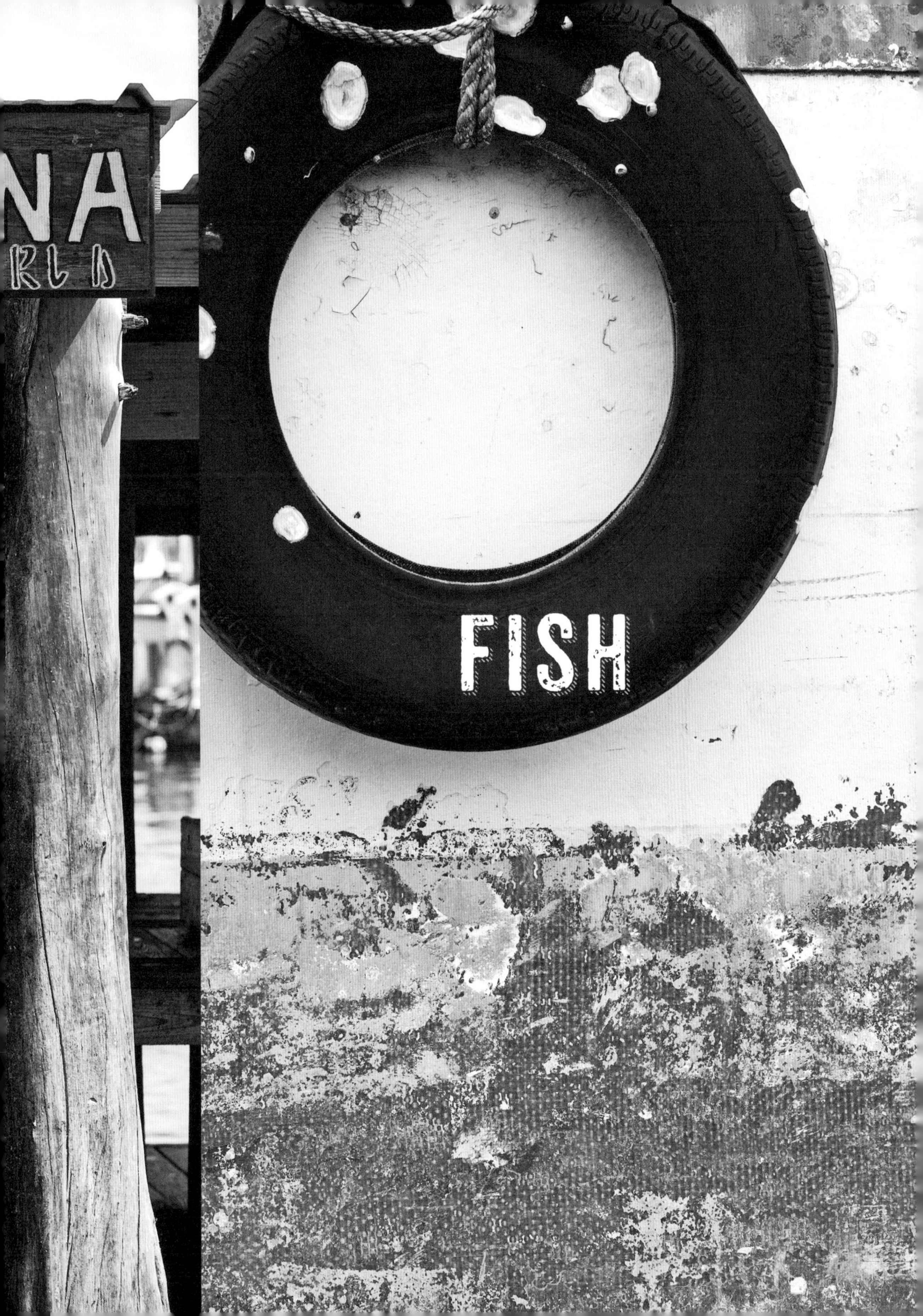

FISH

FISH

GROWING UP IN A FAMILY that loves fishing has been a blessing to me. From the time I could stand, I have been out in the Gulf of Mexico or on the Bogue Chitto River fishing. If I weren't a chef I would without a doubt be a fisherman. There is nothing like being out on the water with the unanswered question of what you might catch.

Through the years, I have become pretty good at it actually, decorating my walls with trophies. I even set a record in the 1984 Grand Isle Tarpon Rodeo children's division with a 3-pound, 4-ounce croaker. I made my father so proud accepting my trophy on stage from Miss Louisiana, even though my shirt was on backwards and inside out.

The boats got bigger and the stakes got higher as we stopped fishing for croakers and started fishing for real game fish, such as tuna and marlin. Eventually we even formed our own hometown fishing team called the "Tylertown Go-getters." The Louisiana coonasses (what we called the locals) would laugh at us Mississippi pine cone pickers (what they called us) launching our boat at the marina in their neck of the woods of Venice, Louisiana. We traveled hours offshore into crystal clear blue water in hopes of catching the "great ole big one," as my dad would say.

Through the years the coonasses's laughter changed to respect as we approached the dock, our coolers overflowing with fish. Once we reached the dock, the disciplined work began of cleaning the boat and butchering the fish. Nowadays my brother and I don't wait to butcher the fish upon return, we bring along a sharp knife to start right away. We are also always armed with a ceviche kit (tomato, jalapeño, lime, cilantro, onion, and sea salt) to enjoy our first catch minutes after it lands in the boat.

RED SNAPPER WITH SATSUMA CHILI SAUCE

SERVES 4

In Louisiana, the red snapper season coincides with the first crop of Louisiana citrus — satsumas. Driving home from successful snapper-fishing excursions, Slade often pulls over at a roadside citrus stand in Plaquemines Parish to pick up a sack of perfectly ripe satsumas for an accompanying sauce. This dish was inspired by the culinary mantra of "what grows together, goes together," referring to the pairing of ingredients that are in season simultaneously. This lovely, mild fish and the sweet, slightly tart satsuma may not "grow" together, but they go together swimmingly.

1 1/2 cups satsuma juice (from about 12 satsuma oranges; clementines are a good substitute)

1 tablespoon sugar

1 tablespoon champagne vinegar

2 tablespoons cold unsalted butter

1 teaspoon ground Aleppo pepper (see Sources, page 223)

4 (5-ounce) red snapper fillets, skin on and boned

1/2 teaspoon fine sea salt

1/2 teaspoon freshly ground black pepper

Wondra flour, for dusting the fish

2 tablespoons extra-virgin olive oil

To make the sauce, in a large saucepan, cook the satsuma juice with the sugar and vinegar over medium-high heat until reduced to a syrupy liquid. Stir in the butter and Aleppo pepper. Keep warm until the fish is cooked.

To cook the fish, season the snapper with salt and black pepper and lightly dust the skin side with Wondra flour to prevent it from sticking to the pan.

In a large sauté pan, heat the olive oil over high heat until it is smoking; decrease the heat to medium-high. Gently lay the fish, one at a time and skin-side down, in the pan; with a flat metal spatula, press the fish firmly until it lays flat.

Continue to cook the fish until the skin is crispy, about 1 minute. You can check the progress by gently lifting the side of the fish and checking the skin side. Once the skin is crispy, turn each fish over and cook just until the tip of a knife feels warm after you poke it though the center, about 1 more minute. Remove the fish from the pan.

To serve, put a pool of sauce in the center of each plate and place the fish on top.

WONDRA FLOUR

Wondra is a brand of instant flour that is precooked and has added barley. This gives it more texture than regular flour, and makes it dissolve instantly. Wondra flour is great for sautéing; it lightly adheres to the surface of a protein to create a nonstick barrier between the meat and the pan, and it yields a crispier, lighter crust.

Pictured with Butter-Glazed Green Cabbage (page 110)

SEARED SCALLOPS IN ANDOUILLE-THYME BUTTER

SERVES 4

A perfectly cooked scallop is cooked just until it is no longer cool in the center and seared to a beautiful caramel color. We have a trick using a two-pronged tool called a meat fork to check the internal temperature: insert the tip of the meat fork half-way down in the center of the scallop, then quickly remove it and place the tip right below your bottom lip. If the metal is just warm, the scallops are a perfect medium. That sweet, perfectly cooked scallop paired with the spiciness of the andouille sausage makes this dish sing. We use dry-packed scallops, which means that they have been naturally packed without the use of a preservative solution that sacrifices flavor and inhibits a golden brown sear.

12 dry-packed jumbo sea scallops

Salt and freshly ground black pepper

5 tablespoons extra-virgin olive oil

2 shallots, finely diced

2 ounces andouille sausage, finely diced

1/2 cup white wine

1/4 cup unsalted butter, diced

1 tablespoon fresh thyme leaves (no stems)

Preheat the oven to 400°F. Heat a large oven-proof sauté pan over high heat until it is smoking. Season the scallops with salt and pepper. Decrease the heat to medium-high, add 2 tablespoon of the olive oil, and place six of the scallops in the pan. Cook the scallops on one side until they are nicely caramelized, about 1 minute. Transfer the cooked scallops to a plate. Repeat this process with the remaining six scallops, removing the old oil and replacing it with 2 tablespoons of the olive oil.

Once the second set of scallops is nicely caramelized on one side, flip them over and add the cooked scallops back to the pan, caramelized side up. Place the pan in the oven for 3 minutes to finish cooking. Transfer all the scallops to a plate.

Remove the old oil from the pan and replace it with the remaining 1 tablespoon of oil. Return the pan to medium heat. Add the shallots and andouille to the pan and cook until the shallots are translucent and soft, about 1 minute. Deglaze the pan with the white wine, scraping the bottom of the pan with a wooden spoon to incorporate all the caramelized bits from the bottom into the sauce.

Cook until the wine is reduced by half; add the butter to the pan. Once the sauce is thick enough to coat the back of a spoon, adjust the seasoning with salt and pepper and stir in the fresh thyme leaves.

Serve the scallops warm with some of the sauce spooned over the top.

SEARED SMOKED PEPPER TUNA WITH MOLASSES-SOY SAUCE

SERVES 4

Who says you can't barbecue fish? In this dish we combine the essential ingredients of great barbecue—smoke, sweet, salt, and vinegar—and pair it with meaty yellowfin tuna. Served with buttery black-eyed peas and green onions, the flavors bring to mind a summer picnic.

1/2 cup molasses

3 tablespoons soy sauce

Scant teaspoon Dijon mustard

1 1/2 teaspoons champagne vinegar

4 (5-ounce) pieces yellowfin tuna, at least
    1 inch thick

2 teaspoons salt

3 tablespoons ground smoked black pepper
    (see Sources, page 223)

2 tablespoons light olive oil

To make the sauce, whisk together the molasses, soy sauce, mustard, and vinegar in a small saucepan. Cook the mixture over medium heat until it's reduced by half, about 5 minutes, skimming the scum completely off of the top of the sauce with a spoon. Let the sauce cool while you cook the fish.

To cook the fish, season each piece of tuna with 1/2 teaspoon of the salt. Pour the smoked pepper onto a plate and spread it out evenly. Gently press each tuna into the smoked pepper on all sides, forming a crust of pepper all over. Tap the tuna pieces lightly to remove any excess pepper.

Heat a large skillet over medium-high heat and add the oil to the pan. Once the oil is almost smoking, sear the tuna on all sides for about 15 seconds each side. This should result in a nice crust, but keep the inside of the fish rare.

Transfer the fish to plates and let cool slightly, then drizzle with the sauce and serve.

ALMOND-DUSTED POMPANO WITH BROWN BUTTER SAUCE

SERVES 4

Pompano is a popular fish found on most menus of New Orleans "old school" restaurants. While trout is generally used in traditional amandine presentations, we think the oily richness and firm texture of pompano work really well with the toasted almond crust. The bright acidity of the brown butter sauce with the addition of fresh parsley makes the classic pairing of these ingredients timeless.

4 (5-ounce) pompano fillets, skinned and boned

1 cup finely ground blanched almonds

Salt and freshly ground black pepper

2 tablespoons light olive oil

1/2 cup unsalted butter, diced

2 lemons, cut into segments and seeded

1 cup loosely packed fresh flat-leaf parsley leaves, finely chopped

1/2 cup chicken stock (page 220)

Heat a dry 12-inch sauté pan over medium-high heat. While the pan is heating, place the ground almonds in an even layer on a flat surface such as a baking sheet. Season the fish fillets on both sides with salt and pepper and lay the fillets on the almonds to coat them on one side.

Add the olive oil to the sauté pan. When the pan is slightly smoking, decrease the heat to medium-low. Add the fillets to the pan, almond side down. Cook the fillets until the almond crust is golden brown, about 2 minutes. Flip the fish in the pan and add the butter, gently basting the fish with spoonfuls of melted butter for 30 seconds. Carefully transfer the fish to a plate. Return the pan to medium-low heat.

Add the lemon segments and stock to the pan, whisking the sauce until it becomes smooth and emulsified. Pass the sauce through a strainer into a small saucepan and cook over medium heat until the stock mixture is reduced to a sauce-like consistency, about 2 minutes.

Remove the sauce from the heat, adjust the seasoning, and stir in the parsley. Spoon the sauce over the fish and serve.

WHITE WINE AND BUTTER–POACHED REDFISH

SERVES 4

Chef Paul Prudhomme popularized redfish back in the eighties with his blackened fish technique. The technique became so popular that redfish became dangerously overfished here on the Gulf Coast. Now, due to strict regulation and sustainable fish farming, the redfish has regained its stature as a staple of the southern Louisiana diet. Redfish is a blast to catch since it puts up quite a fight on the end of your fishing line. This recipe probably couldn't be further from chef Prudhomme's. His is in-your-face spice, ours is a soft whisper of wine and butter and fish that melts in your mouth.

2 tablespoons extra-virgin olive oil

6 shallots, julienned

8 cloves garlic, crushed

3 sprigs thyme

2 fresh bay leaves

1/2 teaspoon salt

1/2 teaspoon freshly ground black pepper

2 cups white wine

1 cup unsalted butter, diced

1 teaspoon honey

1 teaspoon champagne vinegar

4 (6-ounce) redfish fillets, skinned and boned

Fleur de sel, for garnish

To make the sauce, heat the olive oil in a medium saucepan over medium-high heat. Once your pan is smoking, decrease the heat to medium and add the shallots, garlic, thyme, bay leaves, salt, and pepper. Cook the vegetables over medium-low heat until soft and translucent, about 3 minutes. Add the wine, and cook until the wine is reduced by one-third. Over low heat, whisk in the butter, one cube at a time, until all of the butter is incorporated. Strain the sauce into a large sauté pan.

Add the fish fillets to the pan and over low heat, poach the fish on one side for 5 minutes, then, using a spatula, flip the fish over and poach for 5 minutes more.

Serve the fish with some sauce spooned over the top and a sprinkling of fleur de sel.

HALIBUT WITH CREOLE MUSTARD HOLLANDAISE

SERVES 4

Halibut isn't all that common in our neck of the woods, but even so, when it's in season, it's always on the menu. It does require skillful cooking to preserve its moist and flavorful texture. Do not cook halibut with a heavy hand—too aggressive a sear will make it tough. Just go for a very light-brown kiss around the edges. Serve it at its peak, in the spring, with asparagus and this rich and zesty hollandaise.

2 cups unsalted butter, sticks cut into quarters

4 large egg yolks

Juice of 1 lemon

1 tablespoon water

1/2 teaspoon white wine vinegar

1/4 teaspoon fine sea salt

1 tablespoon Creole mustard (see Sources, page 223)

2 dashes hot sauce (our favorite is Crystal's)

2 tablespoons light olive oil

4 (6-ounce) halibut fillets

1/4 teaspoon freshly ground black pepper

To make the hollandaise, place the butter in a small microwave-safe bowl and microwave on high until the butter is completely melted, about 2 1/2 minutes. Remove the butter from the microwave and let it sit for a few minutes, then skim off and discard the foam that has formed on the top. Pour just the clear, yellow butter (clarified butter) into another dish, leaving the milk solids. You will use the clarified butter to make the hollandaise.

In a small saucepan, combine the egg yolks and lemon juice and cook over low heat, whisking the mixture briskly until it starts to thicken. You may need to pull the pan on and off the heat to control the temperature so you do not scramble the egg yolks. Once the eggs are thickened, use a ladle to slowly drizzle half the clarified butter into the eggs while continuing to whisk.

Thin the sauce out a bit with the water to prevent from breaking.

Continue adding the remaining butter and whisking. You should end up with a thick, silky, emulsified sauce. Whisk in the salt, Creole mustard, and hot sauce. Hold the sauce in a warm place like beside the stove (if the sauce gets cool, it will break; if it gets hot, it will break as well), covered with aluminum foil or a lid until you are ready to serve it, up to 30 minutes.

To cook the fish, preheat a large sauté pan over high heat and add the olive oil. Once the pan is almost smoking, decrease the heat to medium and let cool for a minute. Season the halibut fillets with salt and freshly ground black pepper. Gently lay the fillets in the hot pan. Cook for about 1 minute, then turn the fish over. You want a very light browning on each side. Cook for another minute, then remove from the pan to plates. Be careful not to overcook the halibut, as it goes from juicy and moist to dry very quickly.

Serve with the hollandaise on the side.

CHAMPAGNE CATFISH WITH FRENCH TARTAR SAUCE

SERVES 4

In the summer of 1984, I learned the value of a hard-earned buck. I cut grass all summer long at cut-throat rates for my dad's real estate business. After a long hot three months, my piggy bank was full with $130. I bought a remote control boat and immediately took it for a spin out on our three-acre pond. After a couple of hours, I needed a new thrill, so I tied a beetle spin (a type of fishing lure) on the back of the boat with fishing line to catch a bream. As the boat was trolling along the banks of the pond, I was anticipating my first catch. But in a flash I watched my hard-earned money sink into the dark depths of the pond, pulled under by a hungry catfish. After the tears I shed over that boat, I will never underestimate the potential of catfish. If you need more convincing of the boldness of that fish, take a bite of that sneaky bottom-feeder with this over-the-top French tartar sauce, also known as gribiche.

2 tablespoons Dijon mustard

1/4 cup champagne or white wine

4 (6-ounce) catfish fillets, skinned and boned

1/2 cup all-purpose flour

1/2 cup cornmeal

1 tablespoon cornstarch

1 teaspoon Creole spice (page 222)

1/2 teaspoon fine sea salt

1/2 cup canola or other neutral vegetable oil, for frying

French Tartar Sauce (recipe follows)

In a shallow pan, whisk together the mustard and champagne until well mixed. Add the catfish fillets to the pan and coat them well. Marinate the catfish in the mixture in the refrigerator for 30 minutes.

In a blender, combine the flour, cornmeal, cornstarch, Creole spice, and salt. Blend together for 30 seconds to make a fine coating, then pass the mixture through a sifter into a shallow pan.

Remove the catfish from the marinade, shaking off the excess liquid. Place the catfish in the breading mixture and coat evenly on all sides. Shake the excess breading from the catfish.

Heat a large sauté pan with the canola oil over medium-high heat. Once the oil is shimmering and hot, gently lay the catfish fillets in the oil. Cook the catfish on each side until the crust is golden brown, 2 to 3 minutes.

Remove the catfish from the pan and serve with the tartar sauce.

FRENCH TARTAR SAUCE (SAUCE GRIBICHE)

2 large egg yolks

1 tablespoon Dijon mustard

Zest and juice of 1 lemon

1 cup canola oil

1 hard-boiled egg, peeled and finely chopped

5 cornichons, finely chopped

1 1/2 teaspoons capers, drained and finely chopped

1 shallot, peeled and minced

1 tablespoon chopped fresh flat-leaf parsley

1 tablespoon chopped fresh chervil

1/2 teaspoon coarsely ground black pepper

1/4 teaspoon fine sea salt

1/2 teaspoon pepper vinegar (page 222)

1/4 teaspoon hot sauce (we use Crystal's)

Combine the egg yolks, mustard, and lemon juice in a blender and blend until well mixed, about 30 seconds. With the blender on low speed, drizzle the oil into the blender in a very thin stream until the mixture begins to emulsify. Increase the stream of oil slightly, and continue pouring in the rest of the oil, forming a thick mayonnaise. You may need to increase the speed at the very end for 10 seconds to get a thick and fluffy mayonnaise.

Scrape out the mayonnaise from the blender with a rubber spatula and transfer to a small bowl. Add the lemon zest, hard-boiled egg, cornichons, capers, shallot, parsley, chervil, pepper, salt, pepper vinegar, and hot sauce, and fold them into the mayonnaise with the spatula.

This will keep in your refrigerator in an airtight container for up to 1 week.

GRILLED LEMONFISH WITH HORSERADISH SAUCE

SERVES 4

Lemonfish is like our Down South hamachi. Local sushi bars often serve it in place of hamachi, or yellowtail, where it's oily richness benefits from a kick of wasabi. We like to grill it lightly and glaze it with a sauce made with wasabi's more familiar cousin, horseradish. For optimum flavor, when choosing horseradish root, make sure it is nice and firm, not spongy.

2 tablespoons light olive oil

1 small onion, julienned

1 stalk celery, julienned

1 leek, white and light green parts, washed well and julienned

4 cloves garlic, smashed

1 bay leaf

1 sprig fresh thyme

1 cup white wine

1 cup water

1 cup unsalted butter, softened

1 (2-inch) horseradish root, peeled and finely grated

1 1/2 teaspoons salt

4 (6-ounce) lemonfish fillets (also called cobia or lingcod), skinned and boned

1/4 teaspoon freshly ground black pepper

Canola or other neutral vegetable oil, for oiling the grill

To make the sauce, heat the olive oil in a large sauté pan over medium heat. Add the onion, celery, leek, garlic, and bay leaf and cook until soft, about 3 minutes. Add the wine and water and bring to a simmer. Cook the sauce until reduced to about 1/2 cup, then strain it into a small pot.

Place the pot over medium heat and whisk in the butter, 1 tablespoon at a time, until all of the butter is incorporated. Be careful not to add too much butter at once or the sauce will separate.

Remove the sauce from the heat and whisk in the horseradish and the 1 1/2 teaspoons salt. Let the horseradish steep for 10 minutes, then strain the sauce once again through a fine-mesh sieve into a bowl, pressing out all of the juices from the horseradish with a spoon. Discard the horseradish and reserve the sauce.

To cook the fish, be sure your grill (or grill pan) is clean and nicely oiled. Preheat the grill (or grill pan) until nice and hot. Season the fish on each side with salt and pepper. Place the fish on the grill (not on the hottest spot). Grill on one side for 2 minutes, then turn them over and grill them on the other side for 2 more minutes. To check that the fish is cooked medium, insert a meat fork into the center of the fish and then place the tip of the fork right under your lip. If the tip feels just warm, not hot, the fish is perfectly cooked. If it is cold, cook it for a few moments longer.

Serve the fish with the horseradish sauce spooned over it.

BROWN SUGAR–DILL GLAZED SALMON

SERVES 4

Salmon is kind of a sore subject between us. A fan of its silky texture and richness in omega-3s, I always want to put it on the menu. Slade feels that it is a fish prostituted mostly by cruise ships and banquet halls, which have cheapened its reputation. But we both agree that glazed with brown sugar, spicy mustard, and herbaceous dill, this particular salmon is more like a pretty woman.

1¹/2 teaspoons dry vermouth

1 tablespoon champagne vinegar

2 tablespoons light brown sugar

1/2 teaspoon fine sea salt

1/2 teaspoon coarsely ground black pepper

1/4 cup Dijon mustard

3 tablespoons light olive oil

1 teaspoon chopped fresh dill

4 (5-ounce) 1-inch-thick salmon fillets, skinned

Preheat the oven to 350°F.

To make the glaze, combine the vermouth, champagne vinegar, brown sugar, 1/4 teaspoon of the salt, 1/4 teaspoon of the pepper, and mustard in a small mixing bowl. Whisk the ingredients together until they are well incorporated. Slowly drizzle in 2 tablespoons of the olive oil while continuing to whisk to emulsify into the sauce. Fold in the dill. Reserve.

To prepare the salmon, season the fish on both sides with the remaining 1/4 teaspoon salt and 1/4 teaspoon pepper. Heat a large, ovenproof sauté pan over medium-high heat until almost smoking. Decrease the heat to medium and add the remaining 1 tablespoon olive oil to the pan. Place the salmon in the pan and sear the salmon until a nice golden brown forms on the edges, about 1 minute. Turn the fillets to the other side and remove the pan from the heat. Brush each fillet with 1 tablespoon of the glaze.

Bake in the oven until the fish is just warm inside and the glaze is set, 2 to 3 minutes. Transfer the fish to plates and serve with additional glaze alongside.

NEW ORLEANS–STYLE BARBECUE LOBSTER

This is our play on the classic New Orleans dish: barbecue shrimp. It is somewhat of a play on words because you would expect it to be a dish containing barbecue sauce. Instead, it is shrimp cooked in their shells with lots of spice, garlic, and butter in a cast-iron pan, mimicking the elements of a barbecue. We like to use lobster, as the sweetness of lobster meat really comes out with the heat of the Creole spice. Be sure to have a warm baguette on hand to sop up every last drop of sauce.

2 (1¹/2-pound) live lobsters

1 tablespoon light olive oil

2 teaspoons Creole spice (page 222)

2 teaspoons chopped garlic

2 sprigs rosemary

1/4 cup reserved lobster poaching liquid

2 teaspoons Worcestershire sauce

Juice of 2 lemons

1¹/2 cups unsalted butter, cut into 1/2-inch dice

Fill a large saucepan with 4 quarts of water and bring to a boil over high heat.

With your hands, break away the claws and tails from the live lobster's head. Discard the head or save in the freezer for sauce or stock on another day. Cook the claws in the boiling water for 6 minutes, then transfer to a bowl and let cool. Reserve 1/4 cup of the cooking liquid and discard the rest.

To cut up the lobsters and remove the meat, once the lobster claws are cool enough to handle, separate the claws from the knuckles. Place the claws on a cutting board and using the back heel of a chef's knife, whack the claw once firmly, slightly cracking the shell. Wiggle the small pincher until it dislodges from the claw and remove it with the inside cartilidge attached and discard. Break away the cracked shell pieces and pull out the cooked claw meat. Repeat with the remaining claws. Clean the lobster knuckles by inserting kitchen shears

between the meat and the shell, carefully cutting away the shells and using your fingers to open the shell and remove the meat. Reserve all the lobster meat on the side and discard the shells.

On a cutting board, uncurl the tails one at a time with the hard shell side facing up. With a heavy-duty chef's knife, halve the tails lengthwise by placing the tip of your knife at the top and cutting through the middle. Remove the vein that runs through the tail meat and discard. (See photos on pages 166–67.)

To cook the meat, heat a large sauté pan over high heat until smoking, then add the oil. Season the lobster tail meat with 1/4 teaspoon of the Creole spice. Carefully place the lobster tails, cut side down, in the hot pan and decrease the heat to low. Cook the lobster tails for 2 minutes, then turn them and cook for 1 minute more. Add the chopped garlic and rosemary, cooking for 1 minute to soften the garlic. Remove the tails and add the reserved lobster cooking liquid, remaining 1³/4 teaspoons Creole spice, Worcestershire, and lemon juice. Add the butter, a little at a time, whisking until a sauce is formed.

Return all of the lobster to the sauce, warming it for about 1 minute.

Divide the meat between two plates, spoon over the sauce, and serve.

SHRIMP RICHMOND

The first recipe I ever made was Shrimp Richmond, out of the Antoine cookbook that was my father's. It is still one of my favorite cookbooks, beautifully illustrated and full of classic Creole recipes from the century-old New Orleans restaurant. I spent all day in the kitchen making this dish, which was my first lesson in a number of French techniques, such as making velouté, tomato concasse, brunoise of vegetables, gratinée, and my first attempt at a stock. I will never forget my mom's expression as she took her first bite, closing her eyes and savoring the flavor. I felt a bit of chef's pride that night watching my family enjoy what their son had made. Mind you my mom and dad weren't slouches when it came to food, they were well-seasoned New Orleans diners. So garnering their praise over my first attempt at New Orleans cuisine was a healthy nudge towards a career as a chef. This is my version of that dish.

11/2 pounds shrimp (16/20 count), peeled (shells reserved) and cut in 1/2-inch dice

3 cups cold water

1 small tomato, cored and a small X incision cut in the bottom

1/2 cup unsalted butter

1 cup finely diced fennel

1 cup finely diced carrot

1 cup finely diced onion

1 tablespoon finely chopped garlic

1 fresh bay leaf

Sprig of thyme

1/4 cup plus 1 tablespoon all-purpose flour

1/2 cup white wine

1 teaspoon fine sea salt

1/4 teaspoon ground white pepper

1/8 teaspoon cayenne pepper

1 tablespoon chopped fennel fronds

1 tablespoon chopped fresh flat-leaf parsley

1 cup panko (Japanese bread crumbs)

1 cup freshly grated Parmesan cheese

Preheat the broiler.

To make the shrimp stock, place the shrimp shells in a saucepan and cover with the water. Place on medium-high heat and bring to a simmer. Decrease the heat to low and cook for 30 minutes, skimming off and discarding any scum from the surface. Strain the shrimp broth into a bowl and reserve.

Bring a small pot of water to a boil over high heat. Have a small bowl of ice water on the side. Once it has reached a boil, drop in the tomato and cook for about 30 seconds. Remove the tomato from the boiling water and place in the bowl of ice water to stop the cooking. Once the tomato is cool, remove it from the ice water and the peel off the tomato skin and discard it. Cut the tomato into quarters and remove the seeds, discarding them. Chop the tomato flesh finely and reserve.

In a large sauté pan, melt the butter over medium heat. Add the diced fennel, carrot, onion, garlic, bay leaf, and thyme and cook for 3 minutes, stirring occassionally. Add the flour and stir, cooking for 1 minute longer. Whisk in the white wine and 2 cups of the shrimp stock and continue whisking until a thick sauce is formed. Add the salt, white pepper, cayenne pepper, chopped tomato, fennel fronds, parsley, and diced shrimp and continue cooking until the shrimp are just cooked, about 3 minutes.

Pour the mixture into an 1¹/₂-inch-deep ovenproof casserole dish. Mix the bread crumbs with the Parmesan cheese and spread evenly on top of the casserole.

Place under the broiler on the top shelf, watching closely and turning if needed, until the top is golden brown, about 1 minute.

Serve immediately.

GRILLED CALAMARI STUFFED WITH CORNBREAD AND COLLARDS

SERVES 4

Calamari is often prepared like a mozzerella stick, battered, fried, and served with marinara sauce. We aren't knocking the sports bar version, but ours is inspired by a lighter Mediterranean style. Of course, we added Southern soul with the collards and cornbread.

2 1/2 pounds medium calamari

1 pound collard greens, stemmed and washed well

2 cups grated Shallot Cornbread (page 29)

1 tablespoon plus 1 teaspoon chopped garlic

2 ounces pancetta, finely diced

2 teaspoons fine sea salt

1 teaspoon freshly ground black pepper

1/2 cup unsalted butter, melted

3 tablespoons freshly grated Parmesan cheese

Grated zest and juice of 2 lemons

1 teaspoon fresh thyme leaves

1/2 teaspoon red pepper flakes

To prepare the calamari, be sure your grill (or grill pan) is clean and nicely oiled. Preheat the grill (or grill pan) until hot.

Clean the calamari by separating the head from the body. Cut the eyes off of the tentacles and remove the cartilage beak, discarding the eyes and beak. Reserve the tentacles until later.

Remove any membrane from the outside of the body. Using your fingers, pull all of the cartilage out from the inside of the body as well and discard. Chill the bodies and tentacles until you've prepared the stuffing.

To make the stuffing, fill a bowl with ice water and have nearby. In a large saucepan, bring 4 quarts of water with 1/4 cup of kosher salt to a boil over high heat. Once the water is boiling, add the collard green leaves (no stems) and cook until tender, about 3 minutes. Transfer the collard greens to the ice water

bath to cool. Once they are cool, squeeze the excess water from the greens and chop finely.

In a large bowl, mix together the chopped collards, cornbread, 1 tablespoon of the garlic, pancetta, 1 teaspoon of the sea salt, 1/2 teaspoon of the black pepper, 3 tablespoons of the melted butter, Parmesan cheese, half of the lemon juice, and half of the lemon zest. Work the stuffing together with your hands until it starts to come together when squeezed.

Fill each body of calamari two-thirds full of stuffing. Pin the open end closed with a toothpick. In a small bowl, mix together the remaining melted butter with the remaining salt, pepper, garlic, the thyme leaves, and the red pepper flakes to make a butter for basting.

To grill the calamari, place the stuffed bodies on the preheated grill away from the hot spot. Grill, with the cover of the grill closed, for 1 minute on all sides. After the calamari has been on the grill for approximately 5 minutes and has nice grill marks, add the tentacles to the grill. Brush all of the calamari lightly with the garlic butter, cover the grill, and grill for 1 minute more. Remove the calamari from the grill to a platter.

When the calamari are cool enough to handle, remove the toothpicks and slice the bodies into 1-inch-thick rings. Spoon the remaining garlic butter over the calamari and serve.

WINTER STORM

MEAT

MEAT

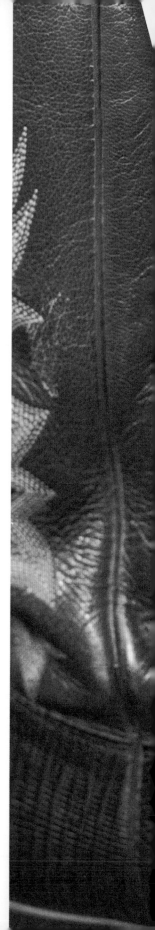

PEOPLE TAKE THEIR MEAT very seriously in this part of the country. One of the reasons may be that the cherished tradition of hunting and bringing home your own meat for the winter continues to be passed down from one generation to the next. Or maybe it's because when you go for a ride out in the country, stopping to let the free-range chickens cross the road is sometimes necessary. Better yet, it could be that men in these parts really like to show off their cooking skills, and nothing does it quite like a glistening pile of meat on the table.

They take it so seriously that if you go to their house, you might not even get it for free, but need to cough up a few bucks for that fried chicken plate. Like at Skip's Patio Inn.

Slade worked with Skip at Mr. B's Bistro in the French Quarter as a young cook. Skip was a calm and confident mentor there, his feathers never ruffled day after day of pumping out nearly three hundred covers every lunch (not that Slade didn't try to piss him off by lighting matches and putting them in the heel of Skip's shoe as he was setting up his station). Nope, he still invited Slade over to the makeshift restaurant that he ran out in his backyard on Sunday afternoons. There were only two options at the Patio Inn, a fried chicken plate or a fried fish plate. But VIP's such as Slade and his fellow cook, Danny, got a lagniappe plate of fried chicken livers, too. They listened to the tunes of Clarence Carter out in that backyard while enjoying a home-cooked meal—but not for free. It cost them five dollars each.

SWEET TEA—ROASTED DUCK IN DATE SAUCE

SERVES 4

Slade and I totally dig Chinese food. On our date nights in New York, we often dined at Congee Village on the Lower East Side or Peking Duck House in Chinatown. So it's fitting that we now present our version of roasted duck at MiLa, but with a sauce that is finished with chewy dates.

BRINE

8 cups freshly brewed black tea (such as Lipton)

8 cups ice water

1 cup sugar

1/2 cup kosher salt

1 1/2 teaspoons black peppercorns

1 1/2 teaspoons red pepper flakes

4 cloves garlic, crushed

2 shallots, thinly sliced

Sprig of thyme

Sprig of sage

Sprig of rosemary

2 bay leaves

1/4 teaspoon cayenne pepper

1 (4-pound) Muscovy duck (neck saved, innards removed and discarded)

4 shallots

2 heads garlic, halved

2 carrots, cut in 1-inch dice

2 stalks celery, cut in 1-inch dice

1 bay leaf

2 sprigs thyme

Sprig of rosemary

Sprig of sage

Freshly ground black pepper

1 cup red wine

1/4 cup brandy

4 cups chicken stock (page 220)

1/4 teaspoon fine sea salt

6 Medjool dates, pitted

2 tablespoons champagne vinegar

1 tablespoon unsalted butter

To brine the duck, combine all the brine ingredients in a small stockpot and add the duck. Place a plate on top of the duck to weight it down. It is important the duck is completely submerged to brine properly. Refrigerate the duck in the brine for 24 hours.

To roast the duck, the next day, preheat the oven to 350°F. Remove the duck from the brine, and place it in a roasting pan surrounded by the reserved duck neck, shallots, garlic, carrots, celery, bay leaf, thyme, rosemary, and sage. Season the duck inside and out with pepper. Roast the duck until an instant-read thermometer inserted into the thick part of the thigh reads 175°F, 1 1/2 to 2 hours. Then remove the duck from the pan and set it aside to cool for 30 minutes. Reserve the vegetables and herbs in the pan to make the sauce.

To make the sauce, place the roasting pan over a burner on medium heat. Deglaze the pan with the red wine and brandy. Using a wooden spoon, scrape the bottom of the roasting pan to release any caramelized bits into the sauce. Cook until the liquid has reduced by half, about 5 minutes. Add the stock and cook for 10 minutes.

Remove the vegetables, herbs, and duck neck from the sauce and discard. Strain the pan sauce through a sieve into a blender; add the salt, dates, vinegar, and butter. Puree until the sauce is smooth and reserve.

Carve the duck and arrange on a platter. Spoon the date sauce over top and serve.

BROWN SUGAR–MARINATED FLANK STEAK

SERVES 4 TO 6

Flank steak is perfect for the summertime grill for many reasons. It has a great flavor, minimal time is required for cooking, it marinates quickly, and, when sliced paper thin, it feeds a crowd. Our marinade does double duty by flavoring the steak and reducing down to a glossy sauce. Serve it with salad when you are in the mood for something light.

1 (1- to 1^1/$_2$-pound) flank steak

1 fresh bay leaf

4 sprigs thyme

10 cloves garlic, crushed

2 tablespoons extra-virgin olive oil

2 tablespoons Dijon mustard

^{1}/$_4$ cup red wine vinegar

^{1}/$_2$ cup packed light brown sugar

2 cups red wine

1 teaspoon fine sea salt

1 tablespoon coarsely ground black pepper

2 tablespoons unsalted butter

To marinate the flank steak, place the steak in 2-inch-deep glass dish. Combine the bay leaf, thyme sprigs, and garlic and distribute over the steak. In a mixing bowl, whisk together the olive oil, mustard, red wine vinegar, brown sugar, and red wine. Pour the marinade over the flank steak to coat and turn the steak to coat the other side as well. Let the steak marinate in the refrigerator for a minimum of 2 hours and a maximum of 4 hours.

Before cooking, be sure the grill is clean and nicely oiled. Preheat the grill until you can barely hold your hand over it.

Remove the steak from the marinade and pat dry. Strain the marinade through a fine sieve into a small saucepan and cook over medium heat until reduced by two-thirds, about 5 minutes. Reserve.

Season the steak on both sides with salt and pepper and place it on the grill. Grill on one side for 3^1/$_2$ minutes, then turn and grill the other side for 3^1/$_2$ minutes, until it's medium-rare. Remove the steak from the grill and let it rest for at least 8 minutes.

While the steak is resting, finish the sauce by whisking in the butter until the sauce is rich and glossy, then keep it warm until you are ready to serve the steak.

To serve the steak, slice it thinly against the grain on the diagonal in ^{1}/$_4$-inch slices. Arrange the slices on a platter and pour the sauce evenly over the steak.

SMOKED RACK OF LAMB WITH TOMATO-JALAPEÑO JAM

SERVES 4

Smoking meat is a task most men love to conquer, but the art of smoking does benefit from some feminine restraint. Aggressive smoke flavor in a dish really kills it—you might as well be chewing on wood chips. The key to this recipe is subtlety. Just a hint of smoke and a touch of sweet tomato jam on the lamb provide perfect harmony on your palate. You will need a stovetop smoker for this recipe and 1 cup of hickory wood chips.

4 (4-bone) lamb racks, about 10 ounces each
    (ask your butcher to French the bones)
1 teaspoon fine sea salt
1 teaspoon freshly ground black pepper
3 tablespoons light olive oil
Tomato-Jalapeño Jam (recipe follows)

Preheat the oven to 450°F. Trim off and discard three of the bones from each rack. Season the racks with salt and pepper.

Place 1 cup hickory wood chips in the smoke box of a stovetop smoker (see Sources, page 223). Place the racks on top of the screen and the chips. Bring the smoker to a full smoke, then shut it off and let lamb steep in smoke for 10 minutes. Transfer the racks to a platter.

Heat a large sauté pan over high heat until smoking. Decrease the heat to medium-high and add the olive oil. Carefully place the racks in the pan, fat side down. Sear the lamb on all sides until golden brown. Place the sauté pan in the oven and cook until it registers 130°F (medium-rare) on an instant-read meat thermometer inserted into the middle of each rack, about 12 minutes. Transfer the racks to a cutting board and let rest for 8 minutes.

To serve, slice each lamb rack into four equal chops. Serve with the jam.

TOMATO-JALAPEÑO JAM

1 pound tomatoes (about 3 large)
1 jalapeño chile, sliced thinly
2 cups sugar
Juice of 1 lemon
1/8 teaspoon fine sea salt
2 tablespoons powdered pectin
1 tablespoon apple cider vinegar

Bring a large pot of water to a boil over high heat. Keep a large bowl of ice water nearby.

With a small paring knife, core the tomatoes and cut an X in the middle of the bottom of each. Once the water reaches a boil, blanch the tomatoes in the boiling water for 1 minute. Drop the tomatoes in the ice water to stop the cooking. Peel the skins off the tomatoes and discard. Cut each tomato into eight wedges.

In a saucepan, combine the tomatoes, chile, 1 cup of the sugar, lemon juice, and sea salt. Bring the mixture to a boil over high heat, stirring occasionally, and let the jam boil for about 2 minutes. Mix together the remaining 1 cup of sugar and powdered pectin. Stir the sugar-pectin mixture into the jam and return to a boil. Cook for 1 more minute, remove it from the heat, and stir in the vinegar. Let the jam cool to set up.

It will keep in the refrigerator for 1 month.

OVERNIGHT PORK SHOULDER WITH POBLANOS AND SATSUMAS

SERVES 8

When Slade was working at Fleur de Sel in New York, he worked with a butcher from Mexico, Maria, who was often in charge of cooking the staff meals. He learned this style of cooking pork with whole pepper and citrus—kind of like Cuban mojo—by watching her. Later, when we were chefs at Jack's, one of our Mexican dishwashers was returning to Mexico permanently, so Jack threw him a going-away party and asked Slade to make the meal. He roasted a whole pig this way, which turned out incredible. This version uses a more manageable cut of meat—pork shoulder. Even better, it cooks while you sleep. Just throw it together and into the oven before bed and let the fragrant aroma of citrus and pork awaken you in the morning.

1 tablespoon fine sea salt

4 teaspoons paprika

2 teaspoons ground cumin

1 teaspoon freshly ground black pepper

1 teaspoon cayenne pepper

1/2 teaspoon ground cinnamon

1 boneless pork shoulder, 5 to 6 pounds

3 poblano chiles, halved and stemmed

1 jalapeño chile, halved and stemmed

3 satsumas, halved

2 leeks, white and pale green parts, halved and washed well

1 carrot, cut in large chunks

1/4 cup coarsely chopped garlic

2 fresh bay leaves

1 tablespoon fresh oregano leaves

4 cups chicken stock (page 220)

Several dozen (6-inch) corn tortillas, warmed, for serving

1 bunch cilantro, leaves only

Preheat the oven to 300°F. To make the rub, mix together the salt, paprika, cumin, black pepper, cayenne pepper, and cinnamon in a small bowl. Evenly rub half of the spice mixture all over the pork shoulder. Place the pork in a roasting pan. Scatter the poblanos, jalapeño, satsumas, leeks, carrot, garlic, bay leaves, oregano, and the remaining spice rub around the meat. Add the stock, cover with waxed paper, and then tightly with aluminum foil. Roast in the oven for 8 hours.

After 8 hours, remove the pan from the oven and uncover. Discard the bay leaves. Transfer the pork to a platter. Puree all of the remaining ingredients in a food processor to make the sauce. Pick the shoulder meat into large chunks and coat with the sauce.

Serve with warm corn tortillas and fresh cilantro leaves.

COFFEE ROASTED PORK LOIN

SERVES 6 TO 8

While the process of brining may seem like a tedious task, requiring a day of advance preparation, the finished product will make you a believer. Pork loin frankly can be bland and tough. Twenty-four hours of a flavorful bath turns swine divine.

BRINE

2 cups hot, freshly brewed coffee

1 cup packed light brown sugar

3 tablespoons kosher salt

1 cup white wine

2 cups ice water

10 cloves garlic, crushed

5 sprigs thyme

1 teaspoon freshly ground black pepper

1 pork loin, around 2 pounds

1 cup panko (Japanese bread crumbs)

1/2 cup finely ground coffee beans

1 teaspoon freshly ground black pepper

2 teaspoons light olive oil

1 tablespoon Dijon mustard

To make the brine, pour the hot coffee into a large bowl. Whisk in the brown sugar and salt until dissolved. Whisk in the wine, water, garlic, thyme, and pepper and let the brine cool. Once the brine is cool to the touch, put the pork loin in the brine. Let the meat sit in the brine, covered, in the refrigerator for 24 hours.

The next day, remove the pork loin from the brine and pat dry with paper towels. Preheat the oven to 350°F.

In a rectangular dish, mix the bread crumbs, ground coffee, and pepper for the crust.

Heat the oil in a large sauté pan over high heat until smoking. Sear the pork loin on all sides until a nice brown crust is formed, about 1 minute on each side. Remove the pork from the pan and let it cool on a plate until it is easily handled. Rub the exterior of the pork evenly with the mustard. Place the pork loin in the crust mixture and coat evenly on all sides.

Place the pork loin in a roasting pan fitted with a wire rack. Roast the pork until the internal temperature registers 145°F on an instant-read thermometer, about 15 minutes.

Transfer the pork to a cutting board and let rest for 10 minutes before slicing and serving. Be sure to reserve the pan juices and pour them over the sliced pork.

DEEP-FRIED TURKEY

SERVES 10, WITH LEFTOVERS

Fried turkey is the answer to a Thanksgiving under the gun. There is no need to wake up at the crack of dawn to put the turkey in the oven. Let that bird brine for 36 hours, then pop it in a cauldron of hot fat (outside, of course). And you've got turkey on the table in under 2 hours. It's not just any turkey. It has juicy meat all over, even the breasts. Don't feel guilty about the frying, you probably only eat turkey once a year. Serve it with a healthy array of sides if that makes you feel better. You'll need to invest in an outdoor turkey frying kit (see Sources, page 223).

3 cups packed light brown sugar

1 1/2 cups Dijon mustard

1/4 cup plus 2 tablespoons salt

2 tablespoons cayenne pepper

2 gallons water

1 bunch thyme

1 head garlic, cloves separated and crushed

1 (10- to 12-pound) turkey

2 1/2 gallons vegetable oil, for frying

Place the turkey in a large food-safe plastic bag inside of an ice chest large enough to contain it. To make the brine, in a large bowl, whisk the brown sugar, mustard, salt, and cayenne pepper until smooth. Gradually whisk in the water, followed by the thyme and garlic and pour around the turkey in the plastic bag, submerging the turkey in the brine. Tie the bag closed, pack the cooler the rest of the way with ice, and brine for 24 hours.

Remove the turkey from the brine and pat dry inside and out with paper towels. Transfer the bird, breast-side up, to a turkey frying basket.

Place the turkey in the frying basket in a 30-quart stockpot and add enough oil to barely cover the bird. Remove the turkey (in the frying basket) from the stockpot and bring the oil to 400°F; this can take up to 1 hour.

Carefully lower the turkey into the hot oil and fry for 3 minutes per pound, about 30 minutes. Lift the turkey in the basket from the fryer and drain over a draining rack for 15 minutes.

Remove the turkey from the basket, carve, and serve.

KING RANCH CHICKEN

SERVES 4

I am sure most families have that one dish that becomes the iconic family favorite. That dish in the Vines' house growing up was King Ranch chicken. There were many nights Mom had to call us to the dinner table more than once to get us there, but not when King Ranch chicken was on the menu. Those nights we were all seated in the kitchen, waiting for dinner to came out of the oven, our senses drenched in its fragrance of cheesy, spicy, chicken-y goodness. Mom beamed with pride as she set the casserole in the middle of the table alongside some jalapeño cornbread. Years after my parents divorced, my dad called Mom to ask if she would please give the recipe for King Ranch chicken to my stepmother, Delores. She, of course, obliged. This is our adapted version of the retro casserole.

1 (3-pound) whole chicken

SALSA
6 tomatillos, husked
1 small onion, quartered
6 cloves garlic
2 jalapeño chiles, stemmed
3/4 teaspoon fine sea salt
1/2 teaspoon freshly ground black pepper
1 tablespoon light olive oil
Juice of 2 limes
1 bunch cilantro, leaves only

SAUCE
1/4 cup unsalted butter
1 red bell pepper, seeded and cut into 1/2-inch dice
1 green bell pepper, seeded and cut into 1/2-inch dice
1 large yellow onion, cut into 1/2-inch dice
1 jalapeño chile, cut into 1/2-inch dice (with seeds)
1 tablespoon chopped garlic
1 teaspoon fine sea salt
1/4 teaspoon paprika
1/4 teaspoon ground cumin
1/4 teaspoon freshly ground black pepper
1/4 teaspoon chili powder
1/4 cup all-purpose flour

4 cups chicken broth (reserved from cooking the chicken)
1/4 cup crème fraîche (page 221)

1 cup vegetable oil
12 corn tortillas
2 1/2 cups crumbled queso blanco (or shredded Jack or Cheddar [Mom's favorite])
1 bunch green onions, white and green parts, thinly sliced

To prepare the chicken and broth, place the whole chicken in a large stockpot and cover with water. Bring the water to a boil over high heat, then decrease the heat to low and simmer for 1 hour, skimming the scum off of the top and discarding as necessary. Once the chicken is cooked, transfer the chicken to a plate to cool and strain the broth, reserving 4 cups to use in the casserole.

Preheat the oven to 350°F.

Meanwhile, make the salsa. Toss the tomatillos, onion, garlic, chiles, salt, pepper, and olive oil in a bowl until the vegetables are well coated. Place the oiled vegetables on a baking sheet and roast in the oven for

30 minutes. Remove from the oven, and place in a food processor with the lime juice and cilantro and pulse the mixture until you get a nice and chunky salsa. Reserve.

To make the sauce, in a large sauté pan over medium-high heat, melt the butter and add the red bell pepper, green bell pepper, onion, chiles, and garlic and cook the vegetables until they have softened, about 5 minutes. Add the salt, paprika, cumin, black pepper, chili powder, and flour, stirring to mix well, and reduce the heat to low. Cook for about 3 minutes. Whisk in the 4 cups reserved chicken broth and the crème fraîche and bring to a simmer over medium heat. Simmer for 10 minutes, then remove from the heat; reserve.

Once the chicken is cool enough to handle, remove the skin, then pull the meat from the bones, discarding bones and skin. Shred the meat and reserve in a bowl.

To soften the tortillas, pour the vegetable oil into a 8-inch skillet and place over medium heat. Once the oil is hot, dip the tortillas in the oil one by one, until they are just soft, about 5 seconds each. Let them drain on paper towels.

To assemble the casserole, butter a 9 by 13-inch casserole dish. Build the casserole as follows, spreading each layer evenly in the dish: half of the tortillas (so they cover the bottom of the dish), then half of the chicken, then half of the pepper sauce, then half of the cheese, and half of the green onions. Repeat. Bake, uncovered, until the cheese is melting and the sauce is bubbly, about 40 minutes.

Remove from the oven, spoon the roasted tomatillo salsa over the top, and serve.

BUTTERMILK FRIED CHICKEN

Serves 6 for dinner (and maybe 2 for cold chicken leftovers)

Fried chicken can really bring out the best or the worst in people, especially when it comes to the last piece. In Rushing family folklore, this exact predicament almost drew blood when my grandparents were out of town. The story goes that my Uncle Reed stabbed my Aunt Gloria in the hand with a fork over the last drumstick. The moral of this gory story is if you make plenty of fried chicken no one has to get hurt.

Note that the chicken must brine for 24 hours before it is cooked.

Brine

1 cup packed light brown sugar

1/2 cup Dijon mustard

11/4 cups kosher salt

2 tablespoons cayenne pepper

3 sprigs thyme

1/2 head garlic, smashed

4 quarts hot water

2 whole chickens, around 3 to 4 pounds each
(preferably organic), each cut into 8 pieces

Flour Mixture

1/4 cup fine sea salt

1 tablespoon freshly ground black pepper

1 tablespoon ground white pepper

2 tablespoons dried thyme

2 tablespoons dried parsley

2 tablespoons mustard powder

5 cups all-purpose flour

Egg Wash

2 cups buttermilk

2 cups heavy cream

3 large eggs

4 quarts peanut oil, for frying

Salt

To brine the chicken, in a bowl large enough to hold the chicken and brine, combine the brown sugar, Dijon mustard, kosher salt, cayenne pepper, thyme, and garlic and mix together thoroughly. Add the 4 quarts hot water, whisking until the sugar and mustard are dissolved in the liquid. Set the bowl of brine over another bowl filled with ice and let cool until the liquid is chilled. Place the chicken parts in the brine, cover, and let sit in the refrigerator for 24 hours.

To make the flour mixture, the next day, combine the salt, black and white peppers, dried thyme, dried parsley, mustard powder, and flour in a large bowl; whisk to blend. Transfer the flour mixture in a durable brown paper bag.

To make the egg mixture, combine the buttermilk, heavy cream, and eggs in a bowl and whisk until combined.

To fry the chicken, fill an 8- to 10-quart, heavy-bottomed saucepan with the peanut oil. Heat the oil over medium-high heat until it registers 360°F on a deep-fry thermometer.

Remove the chicken from the brine and pat dry with paper towels. Place the chicken pieces, one by one, in the egg wash; remove from the egg wash and shake off the excess liquid. Put the chicken pieces, one by one, in the flour mixture in the paper bag and shake well to coat the chicken.

Line a plate with paper towels and have nearby. Once all the chicken is battered and the oil is up to temperature, place the breasts and thighs in the hot oil. Cook for 18 minutes and transfer to the prepared plate. Season the chicken right when it comes out of the oil with salt. Repeat this procedure with the wings and drumsticks and cook for 12 minutes. Transfer the remaining fried chicken pieces to the paper-lined plate and season with salt.

Serve hot, at room temperature, or cold.

CHICKEN THIGHS BRAISED WITH CREOLE MUSTARD

SERVES 4

As perpetually broke cooks, we certainly have eaten more than our fair share of chicken thighs. You can't find a better bang for your buck at the supermarket than thighs, where they run about three dollars for four thighs. It doesn't hurt that with a little coaxing (and braising), the moist dark meat of the chicken thigh will be fall-off-the-bone tender. This recipe is French inspired—with the country mustard, white wine, and a surprise of sweet raisins. It also utilizes celery, an inexpensive and under-appreciated vegetable. Please do not ever throw out the tender tiny yellow celery leaves from the heart of the celery. Finely chopped, they are a lovely addition to the sauce.

4 chicken thighs

1 teaspoon fine sea salt

1/2 teaspoon freshly ground black pepper

1 tablespoon light olive oil

1 large onion, julienned

3 stalks celery, sliced on the diagonal

6 cloves garlic, thinly sliced

1/4 cup raisins

1 fresh bay leaf

Sprig of thyme

Sprig of rosemary

1 cup white wine

2 tablespoons Creole mustard (see Sources, page 223), or any country-style whole-grain mustard

1 cup chicken stock (page 220)

1/2 cup heavy cream

1 tablespoon chopped fresh celery leaves

1 tablespoon chopped fresh flat-leaf parsley leaves

Preheat the oven to 350°F. Season the chicken thighs on both sides with 3/4 teaspoon of the sea salt and all of the ground pepper. Heat an ovenproof sauté pan over medium-high heat and add the olive oil. Once the pan is hot, add the chicken thighs, skin side down, and decrease the heat to medium. Cook the chicken until the skin is a nice golden brown, about 5 minutes. Flip the thighs over and cook for 1 more minute. Remove the chicken from the pan and place on a plate, skin side up.

Add the onion, celery, garlic, raisins, bay leaf, thyme, rosemary, and the remaining 1/4 teaspoon salt to the pan. Cook the vegetables until nice and soft, about 5 more minutes. Increase the heat to medium-high and add the white wine and mustard to the pan. Cook until the wine is reduced slightly, then add the stock and nestle the chicken thighs back into the pan, skin side up. The liquid should not cover the skin.

Cover the pan and braise the chicken in the oven for 25 minutes. Uncover the pan and cook for an additional 20 minutes. Transfer the chicken thighs to a plate. Add the heavy cream to the pan and place it over medium-high heat. Cook until the sauce begins to thicken, about 3 minutes.

Stir in the celery leaves and parsley, spoon the sauce over the chicken, and serve.

GRANDMA SUMMERVILLE'S BURGER

SERVES 6

As a boy, I always looked forward to visiting my Grandma Summerville in West Point, Mississippi. She made these burgers for us on every single visit. Her burger was unique, as was her cooking style in general. One example of this was she used more sugar in her cornbread, being a North Mississippian as opposed to a South Mississipian like us. What is special about these burgers is their their texture—like a country meatloaf that melts in your mouth—and a binding technique similar to making a pâté. We like to eat this burger in a country fashion, between two pieces of thick buttery Texas toast.

1/2 teaspoon salt

1/2 teaspoon freshly ground black pepper

1 teaspoon Worcestershire sauce

1 large egg

3 cannned plum tomatoes, crushed

1/2 cup all-purpose flour

2 1/2 pounds ground beef

1 tablespoon light olive oil

Hambuger buns and your favorite condiments, for serving

In a large bowl, combine the salt, pepper, Worcestershire, egg, tomatoes, flour, and beef together with your hands until thoroughly blended. Divide the mixture into six equal patties. Form the patties into rounds that are 4 inches in diameter and 1/2 inch thick. Chill the patties for at least 30 minutes.

Preheat a griddle (or a heavy, cast-iron pan) on medium heat and coat with the olive oil. Lay your patties on the griddle and cook for at least 5 minutes per side, forming a nice crust on the outside and making sure the patty is hot in the center.

Serve the burgers on your favorite bun with all the fixin's.

GRILLED QUAIL WITH HONEY-SOY BUTTER

SERVES 4

One Sunday after church, Dad was driving my brother and me home on the back country roads of Tylertown, Mississippi. All of the sudden, our Dodge Ram Charger squealed to a stop. We boys didn't know what was going on—until we saw in the middle of the cloud of ensuing dust a covey of quail crossing the road. Dad grabbed the shotgun from the back of the truck, hopped out, and, in his Sunday suit, popped a couple. Later that night, they were simply grilled and served as an appetizer. I still think grilling quail is the way to go, but I embellish it a bit with a shellac of honey and soy.

1 cup unsalted butter, at room temperature

3 tablespoons soy sauce

2 tablespoons honey

1 tablespoon chopped garlic

2 teaspoons red pepper flakes

1 teaspoon sea salt

1 teaspoon freshly ground black pepper

8 semi-boneless quail (rib cages removed for stuffing)

To cook the quail, be sure your grill is clean and nicely oiled. Preheat the grill until nice and hot.

Using a food processor, process the butter with the soy sauce, honey, garlic, and red pepper flakes until dark brown and creamy, about 2 minutes.

Stuff each quail with 1 tablespoon of the butter mixture, and using a pastry brush, brush it all over the skin as well. Season the quail with salt and pepper. Lay each quail, with space between them so they don't touch, around the hottest spot of the grill. Grill on each side for about 30 seconds, constantly brushing the top with the butter mixture before flipping. Repeat this process for about 5 minutes, turning every 30 seconds, until the internal temperature of the quail registers 130°F on an instant-read thermometer, and the skin is lacquered.

Transfer the cooked quail to a platter and brush with the honey-soy butter before serving.

Pictured with Sauté-Steamed Baby Bok Choy (page 114)

VENISON LOIN WITH FOUR SPICES AND RED WINE BACON JUS

SERVES 4

We are always surprised when our guests tell us they never liked venison before they tasted ours. We do love the compliment, but what a shame that so many poor deer are killed twice, first by a gun, then by an overzealous cook. We are speaking of the loin in particular, which when cooked just to medium-rare, is not gamey, but tender and buttery. Game meats are enhanced with the addition of sweetness and aromatic spices. We enjoy using French four spice—a mix of black peppercorns, cloves, nutmeg, and exotic ginger, and the bacon-scented sauce just takes it over the top.

1 (750 ml) bottle dry red wine

3 slices bacon

2 sprigs thyme

3 cloves garlic

2 teaspoons black peppercorns

1 teaspoon whole cloves

1 teaspoon grated nutmeg

1/2 teaspoon ground ginger

11/2-pound venison loin

1 tablespoon light olive oil

2 tablespoons honey

1 teaspoon champagne vinegar

2 tablespoons unsalted butter

Preheat the oven to 400°F.

In a large saucepan over medium heat, combine the wine, bacon, thyme, and garlic and cook until the liquid reduces to 1/2 cup. Strain the reduction into a small saucepan and reserve.

To make the spice rub, using a clean coffee grinder (or one dedicated to grinding spices), grind together the peppercorns, cloves, nutmeg, and ginger until you have a fine powder. Season the venison thoroughly on all sides with the spice rub.

To cook the venison, heat a large sauté pan with olive oil over high heat until it is smoking. Carefully place the venison in the pan and sear it for 1 minute on all sides. Place the pan in the oven and cook until an instant-read thermometer inserted into the thickest part of the venison reads 130°F. Let the venison rest on a wire rack for 5 minutes before slicing.

To make the sauce, heat the red wine reduction over low heat, then add the honey and champagne vinegar. Once the reduction comes to a slow simmer, whisk in the butter and remove the pan from the heat. Slice the venison into 1/4-inch slices and serve with the red wine sauce.

DESSERT

DESSERT

ELIMINATING SUGAR from one's diet is a trend not likely to catch on here in the South. Historically, sugar cane was an important crop here in Louisiana. When I was a kid, my dad would bring home sacks of sugar cane as treats for us to chew on. And if you think that the suggestion of sweetening one's already chilled iced tea with a packet of granulated sugar, instead of sweetening before chilling so the sugar melts, couldn't possibly make a Southern lady curse you out, think again.

Nope, our sweet tooths are here to stay. But sugar isn't the only crop down here we have to work with for finishing a meal. We have Ponchatoula strawberries, Ruston peaches, a variety of Plaquemines Parish citrus, Mississippi apples, pick-your-own blueberry farms, and a couple of local fig varieties at our fingertips.

Personally, I lean towards tropical fruit like coconut. I always looked forward to my Papaw Jack's birthday because he insisted on not one, but two coconut desserts every year—coconut cake and coconut cream pie. Slade and I made our own wedding cake that was inspired by the classic Southern coconut-and-citrus holiday dessert, ambrosia. We pulled it together the night before the wedding—layers of rum-soaked cake with pineapple pastry cream, frosted with coconut buttercream and toasted coconut, and finished off with candied citrus and cherries from Fauchon. Word traveled fast through our small group of guests that we made the cake, and I was approached every few minutes about cutting the cake already. I gave up and cut the cake early. Down South, dessert just can't wait.

MUSCADINE WINE JELL-O WITH TROPICAL FRUIT AND CREAM

SERVES 6

As a child, when I was sick enough to miss school, my mom would always take me to my papaw Parker's house. I loved being alone with him reading his copies of *Reader's Digest* as he waited on me hand and foot. To my delight, he always served me Jell-O with fruit cocktail suspended inside the wobbly cubes, finished off with a dollop of Cool Whip. This gelée is my grown-up version of that dish, dedicated to the memory of the one of the sweetest men I have ever known.

3 sheets gelatin

1 (375 ml) bottle muscadine wine (we use Amato's)

1 cup simple syrup

Pinch of salt

1 cup heavy cream

2 tablespoon confectioners' sugar

2 kiwifruit, skinned and thinly sliced

1 mango, skinned and thinly sliced around the pit

2 leaves fresh mint, finely julienned

In a bowl of ice water, soak the gelatin sheets until soft, about 3 minutes.

Combine the muscadine wine, simple syrup, and salt in a saucepan and heat over medium heat until it is steaming, but not boiling. Remove from the heat.

Remove the gelatin sheets from the ice water and squeeze them until all of the water is extracted. Place the gelatin in the muscadine wine mixture and stir until the gelatin is just dissolved. Divide the mixture equally among your serving dishes, we use 8-ounce soup bowls and refrigerate on a completely flat surface until set, about 8 hours.

Right before you're ready to serve the dish, whip the cream on medium-high speed in a stand mixer fitted with a whisk attachment, until soft peaks begin to form. Add the confectioners' sugar and continue whipping until the mixture stands in stiff peaks when you lift the whisk from the bowl, being careful not to overwhip the cream.

To assemble the dish, place three slices of kiwi and three slices of mango on each gelée. Top each gelée with a spoonful of whipped cream and a few strands of mint.

Note: Muscadine is a sweet wine made with Southern muscadine grapes. A sweet Riesling will substitute if you can't find muscadine.

BANANA PUDDING BRÛLÉE

SERVES 4

We opened our former restaurant, the Longbranch, about a week after Hurricane Katrina. Pushing forward with a fine dining restaurant while there were people living in tents down the street was emotionally disconcerting, to say the least. We created this dessert around that time, evoking the memories of our childhood banana puddings made with Nilla wafers and whipped cream. We desperately needed comfort and our trickling stream of guests did, too.

4 egg yolks

1/2 vanilla bean

1/4 cup plus 1 tablespoon granulated sugar

1 teaspoon banana liqueur

4 cups heavy cream

2 tablespoons confectioners' sugar

1 banana, peeled and cut diagonally into
   1/4-inch slices

4 tablespoons turbinado sugar

Cats' Tongues Cookies, for accompaniment
   (recipe follows)

Preheat the oven to 325°F.

Put the egg yolks in a bowl. Split open the vanilla bean and scrape out the seeds with the back of a knife into the bowl with the yolks. Whisk until incorporated. Add the granulated sugar and whisk until smooth. Immediately add 2 cups of the heavy cream and the banana liqueur, again whisking until everything is well combined. Pour the mixture into four 6-ounce ramekins.

Arrange the ramekins in a deep, ovenproof casserole dish. Add hot water to the casserole dish until it reaches halfway up the sides of the ramekins. Tightly cover the casserole dish with aluminum foil and bake for 45 minutes.

Carefully remove the casserole dish with the ramekins from the oven and remove the foil, being careful of the steam. Transfer the ramekins to a baking sheet to cool. Once they are cool enough to handle, chill the ramekins in the refrigerator until they are set and cold, at least 2 hours.

Just before serving, make the sweetened whipped cream. In a stand mixer fitted with the whisk attachment, or with a handheld whisk, whip the remaining 2 cups cream until it almost forms a soft peak. Add the confectioners' sugar and whip until you have soft peaks.

To finish the brûlées, place three slices of banana on each serving, then evenly sprinkle each with 1 tablespoon of turbinado sugar; tap off the excess sugar. Using a kitchen torch (or place the brûlées under the broiler), melt and caramelize the sugar until a nice crunchy top is formed. Top with sweetened whipped cream and cookies.

CATS' TONGUES COOKIES

1/2 cup unsalted butter, at room temperature

3/4 cup granulated sugar

1/4 teaspoon salt

4 large egg whites, at room temperature

1 teaspoon pure vanilla extract

3/4 cup all-purpose flour, sifted

Preheat the oven to 375°F. Line two baking sheets with parchment paper.

In the bowl of an electric mixer fitted with the paddle attachment, beat the butter, sugar, and salt at medium speed until well-blended and light, about 1 minute. Decrease the speed to low and add the egg whites, beating well and scraping down the sides. Add the vanilla extract and fold in the sifted flour, blending well.

Spoon the batter into a pastry bag fitted with a number 2 tip. Pipe the batter onto the prepared sheets in small circles, about 2 inches apart. Bake the cookies, one sheet at a time, until golden brown around the edges, 7 to 10 minutes. Cool on a rack for 10 minutes.

RICE PUDDING WITH RUM RAISINS

SERVES 4

Slade created this recipe at Longbranch through much trial and error. He found that cooking the rice first in water and rinsing away the excess starch results in a creamy, never grainy texture. The tonka bean, the seed of the South American Cumaru tree used in the perfume industry, adds a fragrance with notes of caramel and licorice. Using short-grain Japanese rice produces a dense toothsome pudding, and the rum-soaked raisins are inspired by his favorite flavor of Haagen-Dazs.

RUM RAISINS

1 cup golden raisins

1/2 cup dark rum

1/4 cup sugar

Water

RICE PUDDING

8 cups water

Pinch of salt

4 ounces short-grain rice (we use Japanese rice)

1 3/4 cups milk

1 cup heavy cream

1 vanilla bean, split and scraped, seeds reserved

1 tonka bean (optional, see Sources, page 223)

1/2 cup sugar

2 large egg yolks

To prepare the raisins, combine the raisins, rum, and sugar in a small saucepan and add enough water to cover. Cook on low heat until the raisins are nice and plump, about 5 minutes. Remove from the heat and reserve.

To make the pudding, in a saucepan, bring the water to a boil with a pinch of salt. Whisk in the rice and return to a simmer. Cook until the rice is cooked through, about 14 minutes. Strain the rice into a colander, and return it to the same saucepan along with the milk, heavy cream, the vanilla bean pod and seeds, and the tonka bean. Bring back up to a simmer.

Meanwhile, in a bowl, whisk together the sugar and the egg yolks until smooth; whisk some of the hot rice mixture into the egg mixture to temper. Return the tempered yolks to the rice mixture and cook, stirring with a wooden spoon, until the cream coats the back of a spoon, about 6 minutes.

Fill a large bowl with ice. Pour the rice pudding into a bowl and rest on the ice to cool quickly. Remove the tonka bean and the vanilla bean pod and discard.

Once cool, serve the rice pudding garnished with the rum raisins and their liquid on top.

DELORES'S APPLE CAKE

SERVES 12

The first time Slade met my family in North Louisiana was also our first Christmas together. We stayed at my father's house in Farmerville and were stuck inside due to a severe ice storm. It was a perfect excuse to bake, so my stepmom, Delores, nervously made Slade her apple cake for the first time. Little did she know that he would get up in the middle of the night to eat it and find that future brother-in-law, Jason, was already there. What makes this cake so irresistible is its chewy and moist texture that lasts for days (and nights).

2 teaspoons pure vanilla extract

2 large eggs, well beaten

11/2 cups vegetable oil

Juice of 1/2 lemon

1 teaspoon salt

1 teaspoon ground cinnamon

2 cups sugar

3 cups all-purpose flour

11/4 teaspoons baking soda

3 green apples, peeled and diced in 1/8-inch dice (about 3 cups)

11/2 cups pecans, toasted and chopped

Confectioners' sugar, for garnish

Preheat the oven to 350°F. Butter and flour a 10-cup bundt pan and set aside.

Combine the vanilla, eggs, oil, and lemon juice in a large bowl and whisk thoroughly. Whisk the salt, cinnamon, and sugar into the oil mixture until combined. In a separate bowl, whisk together the flour and baking soda. Add the flour mixture to the oil-sugar mixture and whisk until combined. You should have a very thick batter. Fold the diced apples and toasted pecans into the batter with a spatula until thoroughly mixed. Spread the cake batter in the prepared bundt pan.

Bake the cake until a toothpick inserted into the cake comes out clean, about 11/4 hours.

Let the cake cool for 10 minutes, then turn it out onto a serving platter. Just before serving, garnish it with a sprinkling of confectioners' sugar.

SUMMER GINGER-PEACH TRIFLE

Serves 12

As a young girl in North Louisiana, summertime for me meant Ruston peaches and the Ruston peach festival. My family traveled every year to that town, 45 minutes away, to indulge in those sweet juicy peaches prepared a hundred ways. My dad also made his signature homemade peach ice cream when the peaches were at their prime. These days when I get my hands on peaches at their seasonal best, I go for a show-stopping dessert, such as this ladylike ginger-laced trifle.

Ginger Pound Cake

2 tablespoons minced candied ginger

3/4 cup granulated sugar

1/4 cup packed brown sugar

1/2 cup unsalted butter, diced, at room temperature

11/2 cups cake flour

1/2 teaspoon baking powder

1/4 teaspoon baking soda

1/2 teaspoon salt

2 large eggs

1/2 cup sour cream

1 teaspoon pure vanilla extract

Vanilla Pastry Cream

5 cups heavy cream

1 vanilla bean, pod split, seeds scraped, and
   pod discarded

4 large egg yolks

1/2 cup granulated sugar

3 tablespoons cornstarch

Poached Peaches

Juice of 1 lemon

2 tablespoons brandy

4 ounces fresh ginger, peeled and sliced 1/8 inch thick

2 cups granulated sugar

4 cups water

2 quarts peaches, fruit pitted and cut into
   6 wedges each

Candied ginger, julienned, for garnish

Preheat the oven to 350°F. Line a baking sheet with parchment paper and spray with nonstick cooking spray.

To make the cake, in a stand mixer fitted with a paddle attachment, beat the candied ginger, granulated sugar, brown sugar, and butter on medium speed until the mixture is light and fluffy. In a separate bowl, whisk together the flour, baking powder, baking soda, and salt. In a separate bowl, whisk together the eggs, sour cream, and vanilla extract until nice and smooth.

Starting with the dry ingredients, add them alternately with the wet ingredients (ending with dry ingredients) to the mixer bowl on low speed, stopping to scrape down the bowl occasionally.

Using a spatula, spread the cake batter in the baking sheet and smooth with a spatula into an even layer. Bake for 12 minutes, turning the pan halfway through the cooking. The cake is done when a toothpick inserted in the center comes out clean. Set aside on a rack in the pan to cool.

To make the pastry cream, in a stand mixer with the whisk attachment, whip 1 cup of the cream on high speed until stiff peaks form. Reserve the whipped cream in the refrigerator.

In a small saucepan, combine the remaining 4 cups heavy cream and the vanilla bean seeds and scald the mixture (a skin forms on top) over medium-high heat. Remove the cream from the heat.

Fill a bowl with ice and have nearby. In a bowl, combine the egg yolks, granulated sugar, and cornstarch; whisk together until a thick yellow paste is formed. Immediately, slowly whisk the hot cream mixture into the egg yolks until both are fully combined. Return the cream-egg mixture to the saucepan and cook over medium heat, stirring constantly with a wooden spoon, until the cream reaches a pudding-like consistency. Pour the hot cream into a bowl and rest on the ice, stirring the cream mixture until it is cool.

Once the pastry cream is cool, fold in the whipped cream in three additions with a rubber spatula. Refrigerate the pastry cream until you are ready to assemble the trifle.

To prepare the peaches, in a large saucepan, combine the lemon juice, brandy, fresh ginger, granulated sugar, water, and peaches and place over medium-high heat. Stir the mixture periodically to make sure the sugar is dissolving. Once the peaches reach a slow simmer, cook them until the peaches are fork-tender, about 8 minutes. Remove the peaches from the heat, and strain the syrup through a colander. Save both the peaches and the syrup separately, but discard the ginger pieces. Let them cool before assembling your trifle.

To assemble the trifle, using a round trifle mold as a guide, invert it on the cake and cut out two 8-inch rounds. Place one cake round in the bottom of the trifle mold. Using a pastry brush, brush the cake layer well with the peach syrup. Add one-third of the pastry cream and smooth it evenly over the cake. Arrange half of the sliced peaches evenly over the pastry cream. Repeat the process once more: the second cake round, one-third of the pastry cream, and the remaining peaches. Top the trifle with the remaining pastry cream and smooth evenly over the top. Garnish with julienned strips of candied ginger.

PECAN PRALINE SEMIFREDDO WITH BOURBON CARAMEL

SERVES 10

Pecan pralines are one of the most celebrated candies of the South. They are made with pecans, sugar, and cream, which results in a unique crystallized and cloudy caramel that melts in your mouth. The European praline, however, is made simply with sugar and nuts, which results in a shiny, hard-crack bitter-and-sweet candy. This Italian-style semifreddo (half frozen) uses the latter, which holds up well when frozen. However, we still use cream, but in a soft, fluffy base that cradles the crispy praline.

PECAN PRALINE

1/4 cup water

1 cup sugar

2 cups toasted pecan halves

PARFAIT BASE

3 cups heavy whipping cream

1 cup sour cream

4 large eggs, separated, at room temperature

1/2 cup sugar

BOURBON CARAMEL

1/3 cup water

1 cup sugar

3/4 cup heavy cream

1 tablespoon bourbon

To make the praline, line a baking sheet with waxed paper.

Combine the water and the sugar in a saucepan over high heat. Gently swirl the pan around to melt the sugar evenly. Using a candy thermometer, cook the sugar until it reaches 370°F. Add the pecan halves to the caramel and quickly stir the nuts to coat them thoroughly with the caramel. Spoon the praline onto the waxed paper in an even layer to cool. Once the praline has cooled, chop it finely with a knife and reserve.

To make the parfait, line a 9 by 5 by 3-inch loaf pan with plastic wrap, letting enough excess wrap hang over the sides to cover the top.

Using a stand mixer fitted with the whisk attachment, whip the heavy whipping cream on medium-high speed until it reaches stiff peaks. Remove the bowl from the mixer and, with a rubber spatula, fold the sour cream into the whipped cream. Transfer the mixture to a large bowl and refrigerate until needed.

Have the egg yolks and egg whites in separate bowls. Put the egg yolks in a stand mixer fitted with the whisk attachment and add 1/4 cup of the sugar. Whisk the mixture on high speed until you achieve a thick, pale yellow consistency. Transfer the mixture to another bowl and reserve.

Using a stand mixer fitted with the whisk attachment, whisk the egg whites on medium speed until frothy. Decrease the speed to low and slowly sprinkle the remaining 1/4 cup sugar into the whites. Once the sugar is added, increase the speed to high and whisk until medium peaks form.

CONTINUED

Fold the cream mixture into the yolks, then fold in the egg whites in three additions. Fold in the chopped pecan praline.

Fill your prepared loaf pan with the semifreddo mixture and smooth out the top. Pull the plastic wrap over the top and freeze for at least 4 hours, but preferably overnight.

To make the caramel, using a candy thermometer, cook the water and the sugar in a medium saucepan over medium-high heat until it reaches 380°F. Remove the caramel from the heat and carefully add the heavy cream. Return it to the stove over low heat. Once the cream dissolves into the caramel, you need to swirl the pan periodically but try not to stir it, remove it from the heat and add the bourbon. Hold the caramel at room temperature until you are ready to serve it.

To serve the semifreddo, pull the plastic wrap away from the top. Invert the loaf pan onto a platter. Wrap a hot, wet kitchen towel over the loaf pan and gently rub the sides to release the semifreddo. Once the semifreddo is released onto the platter, peel off the plastic wrap.

Slice the semifreddo into ten equal slices with a sharp knife. Serve each with a drizzle of bourbon caramel.

CHOCOLATE CROISSANT BREAD PUDDING

SERVES 8

Finishing a meal on a good note is easy when you serve a warm chocolate dessert. Selecting a good dark chocolate is the most important step in making this pudding. An easy brand to find is Scharffen Berger 70 percent bitterweet bars. If you can't find that particular brand, choose a dark chocolate in the range of 65 to 70 percent cacao. Serve this bread pudding warm with your favorite vanilla ice cream and listen to the room go silent as your guests dig in.

4 cups heavy cream

2 1/2 pounds dark chocolate (see headnote), cut into small pieces

1 1/4 cups granulated sugar

16 large egg yolks

2 tablespoon good-quality dark cocoa powder

8 croissants, cut into 1/2-inch pieces

Preheat the oven to 325°F. Butter a 9 by 13-inch ovenproof baking dish.

In a medium saucepan, scald the heavy cream (a skin forms) over high heat. Remove from the heat. Place the chocolate in a large bowl and pour the hot cream over the chocolate. Whisk the chocolate into the cream until it is fully melted.

In a separate large bowl, whisk together the sugar, egg yolks, and cocoa powder until smooth. Slowly whisk the chocolate cream

mixture into the sugar-egg yolk mixture until fully incorporated. Add the croissant pieces and stir until they are well coated in chocolate. Let the bread soak in the chocolate for at least 30 minutes, stirring well every 10 minutes.

Pour the pudding into the prepared baking dish and spread it out evenly. Cover the dish tightly with aluminum foil and place it in the center of a large roasting pan. Place the pan in the oven and, using a pitcher, pour hot water into the roasting pan until the water is halfway up the sides of the pudding dish.

Bake, covered, for 30 minutes. Remove the foil, and bake, uncovered, an additional 30 minutes. Remove the pudding from the water bath and let cool for at least 10 minutes before serving.

GOAT'S MILK FROZEN YOGURT WITH WINE-GLAZED BLACKBERRIES

SERVES 4

Slade's hometown of Tylertown, Mississippi, has recently resurrected its dairy industry past, but with goats instead of cows. Ryals Dairy sells their velvety goat cheeses and yogurt at the market here in New Orleans each week. Slade is enamored with the yogurt, which he turns into this refreshing frozen dessert during our endless summer. The red wine–glazed blackberries add a little sophistication to this small town yogurt.

FROZEN YOGURT

1/8 teaspoon salt

1/4 teaspoon fresh squeezed lemon juice

1 tablespoon corn syurp

1 cup simple syrup

16 ounces plain goat's milk yogurt

GLAZED BERRIES

1/2 cup red wine

1/4 cup sugar

8 ounces fresh blackberries

To make the frozen yogurt, whisk the salt, lemon juice, corn syrup, simple syrup, and yogurt together in a large mixing bowl. Freeze the yogurt in a ice cream machine following the manufacturer's instructions. Store the frozen yogurt in the freezer until you are ready to serve it.

Meanwhile, to prepare the berries, in a small saucepan over medium-high heat, cook the red wine and the sugar together until the liquid reduces and becomes syrupy. Add the blackberries to the reduction and gently stir until the berries are soft and glazed, about 3 minutes. Remove the pan from the heat and let the blackberries cool.

Serve the frozen yogurt topped with spoonfuls of wine-glazed berries.

BASICS

BASICS

VEGETABLE STOCK

Makes 8 cups

1 large carrot
1 large onion
2 stalks celery
2 cloves garlic
1 fresh bay leaf
Sprig of thyme
10 cups water

Add all of the ingredients to a large saucepan and simmer, uncovered, for 30 minutes. Strain and let cool.

Keep covered in the refrigerator for up to 2 weeks, or up to 6 months in the freezer.

MUSHROOM STOCK

Makes 8 cups

1 pound button mushrooms (or assorted mushroom stems, or a combination of stems and button mushrooms)
10 cups water

Wash the mushrooms well and place in a large saucepan. Cover with the water and bring to a boil over high heat. Decrease the heat to a slow simmer and cook, uncovered, for 1 hour, or until it is dark and richly flavored. Strain and chill.

The stock keeps in the refrigerator in an airtight container for 2 weeks, or in the freezer for up to 6 months.

CHICKEN STOCK

Makes 10 cups

1 pound chicken wings
12 cups cold water
1 small onion
1 small carrot
1 stalk celery
1 bay leaf
2 cloves garlic, crushed

Place the chicken wings in a 4-quart saucepan and cover with the cold water. Bring to a boil over high heat, then decrease the heat to a simmer. Skim off all of the impurities from the surface and discard (this should take about 5 minutes). Once there are no more impurities, add the onion, carrot, celery, bay leaf, and garlic and cook gently for 1 hour. Strain and cool immediately.

The stock keeps in the refrigerator in an airtight container for 1 week, or in the freezer for up to 6 months.

HOMEMADE MAYONNAISE

MAKES 1/2 CUP

2 large egg yolks
1 teaspoon freshly squeezed lemon juice
1/2 teaspoon grated lemon zest
1 teaspoon champagne vinegar
1/2 teaspoon Dijon mustard
1/2 cup canola or other neutral vegetable oil
Salt and freshly ground black pepper

Combine the egg yolks, lemon juice and zest, champagne vinegar, and mustard in a bowl set over a larger bowl filled with ice. Using a small whisk, mix together thoroughly and then slowly whisk in the oil in a slow, steady drizzle until all of the oil is incorporated. The result should be a thick emulsification. Season with salt and pepper.

Keep the mayonnaise refrigerated until needed. If you don't plan on using the mayonnaise right away, it keeps in an airtight jar in the refrigerator for up to 1 week.

CRÈME FRAÎCHE

MAKES 2 CUPS

2 cups heavy cream
1 tablespoon buttermilk

In a small bowl, whisk together the cream and buttermilk and cover with cheesecloth. Let the mixture stand at room temperature for 48 hours. Discard the cheesecloth and remove the skin that has formed on top of the cream, discarding it as well.

The crème fraîche will keep, in a covered container in your refrigerator, for up to 2 weeks.

GARLIC CONFIT

MAKES ABOUT 1 CUP

24 garlic cloves, peeled
1 cup light olive oil

To make the confit, place the peeled garlic cloves in a small saucepan and cover with the olive oil. Cook over very low heat, being careful not to color the garlic, until it is soft, about 30 minutes. Strain out and discard the oil, and reserve the garlic cloves.

The confit will keep in an airtight container in the refrigerator for up to 1 week.

CREOLE SPICE

Makes about 1/4 cup

1 tablespoon fine sea salt
2 teaspoons white pepper
1 3/4 teaspoons cayenne pepper
1 teaspoon freshly ground black pepper
1 3/4 teaspoons garlic powder
1 1/2 teaspoons onion powder
1 teaspoon dry mustard
1/2 teaspoon ground cumin

In a small bowl, whisk together all the ingredients until they are thoroughly mixed.

The spice mix will keep in an airtight container in the pantry for up to 6 months.

CHILI OIL

Makes 1 cup

1 tablespoon sliced garlic
2 tablespoons red pepper flakes
1 cup light olive oil

Combine the garlic, red pepper flakes, and oil to a small saucepan and place over medium-low heat. Let the oil come to a slow bubble and cook for 5 minutes. Remove from the heat, let the oil cool for 5 more minutes, and then strain through a fine sieve and reserve.

PEPPER VINEGAR

Makes about 2 cups

1 cup fresh Thai chiles (but any hot pepper will do—they just vary in heat)
2 cups apple cider vinegar
1/8 teaspoon salt
1/8 teaspoon sugar

Rinse the chiles in cold water to remove any dirt. Place them in a 1-quart jar with a tight-fitting lid.

Heat the vinegar, salt, and sugar in small saucepan over high heat until the liquid reaches a boil. Pour the hot vinegar over the chiles and let cool to room temperature. Cover and refrigerate for at least 48 before using.

The vinegar keeps for up to 1 month in the refrigerator.

SOURCES

Aleppo pepper, smoked black pepper,
licorice root, tonka bean
   www.gourmetspicecompany.net

Coconut puree
   www.baldor.com

Creole mustard
   www.cajungrocer.com

Stovetop smoker
   www.surlatable.com

Tabasco Spicy Pepper Jelly
   www.cajungrocer.com

Truffle puree and truffle oil
   www.urbani.com

Turkey frying kit
   www.cajungrocer.com

ACKNOWLEDGMENTS

Our heartfelt thanks go out to:

Our families, with a special thanks to Ralph and Delores, Doug and Joan, Heath and Amanda, and Howard and Ruby for their hospitality on location

Our mentors: Mike Anthony, Daniel Bonnot, Alain Ducasse, Didier Elena, Bruce Hill, Jack and Grace Lamb, Gerard Maras, Wayne Nish, Cyril Renaud, and Alain Rondelli

Our agent, Sharon Bowers at the Miller Agency

Our team at Ten Speed: Jenny Wapner, Emily Timberlake, and Betsy Stromberg

Our photographer, Ed Anderson

Our prop stylist, Angie Mosier

Our friend Lolis Elie, for getting us back on the cookbook horse

Our boss, Frank Zumbo

Our staff at MiLa: Dolly, Godfrey, Harry Johnson II, Henry, Hung, Jake, James, Jeff, Jon, Lauren, J. Lorraine, Marcel, Michael, Nick, Paulette, Picayune, Rigo, Scott, Stephen, T, and Wes

Our most cherished vegetable farmers, Luther and Joyce Johanningmeier

Our hometown goat cheese makers, Bill and Blake Ryals

Our Mississippi sausage man, John Fortenberry

Our esteemed family shoemaker, Roy Rushing, in Ferriday, Louisiana

Our favorite stove, Blue Star Range

INDEX

MEASUREMENT CONVERSION CHARTS

VOLUME

U.S.	Imperial	Metric
1 tablespoon	1/2 fl oz	15 ml
2 tablespoons	1 fl oz	30 ml
1/4 cup	2 fl oz	60 ml
1/3 cup	3 fl oz	90 ml
1/2 cup	4 fl oz	120 ml
2/3 cup	5 fl oz (1/4 pint)	150 ml
3/4 cup	6 fl oz	180 ml
1 cup	8 fl oz (1/3 pint)	240 ml
1 1/4 cups	10 fl oz (1/2 pint)	300 ml
2 cups (1 pint)	16 fl oz (2/3 pint)	480 ml
2 1/2 cups	20 fl oz (1 pint)	600 ml
1 quart	32 fl oz (1 2/3 pint)	1 l

TEMPERATURE

Fahrenheit	Celsius/Gas Mark
250°F	120°C/gas mark 1/2
275°F	135°C/gas mark 1
300°F	150°C/gas mark 2
325°F	160°C/gas mark 3
350°F	180 or 175°C/gas mark 4
375°F	190°C/gas mark 5
400°F	200°C/gas mark 6
425°F	220°C/gas mark 7
450°F	230°C/gas mark 8
475°F	245°C/gas mark 9
500°F	260°C

LENGTH

Inch	Metric
1/4 inch	6 mm
1/2 inch	1.25 cm
3/4 inch	2 cm
1 inch	2.5 cm
6 inches (1/2 foot)	15 cm
12 inches (1 foot)	30 cm

WEIGHT

U.S./Imperial	Metric
1/2 oz	15 g
1 oz	30 g
2 oz	60 g
1/4 lb	115 g
1/3 lb	150 g
1/2 lb	225 g
3/4 lb	350 g
1 lb	450 g

Copyright © 2012 by Allison Vines-Rushing and Slade Rushing
Photographs copyright © 2012 by Ed Anderson

All rights reserved.
Published in the United States by Ten Speed Press, an imprint of the
Crown Publishing Group, a division of Random House, Inc., New York.
www.crownpublishing.com
www.tenspeed.com

Ten Speed Press and the Ten Speed Press colophon are registered
trademarks of Random House, Inc.

Library of Congress Cataloging-in-Publication Data

Vines-Rushing, Allison.
  Southern comfort : a new take on the recipes we grew up with /
Allison Vines-Rushing, Slade Rushing.
      p. cm.
  Summary: "The much-anticipated debut cookbook from two of the
most admired and innovative young chefs in the South, with 100 reci-
pes featuring their refined, classically-inspired takes on the traditional
Southern food they grew up with" — Provided by publisher.
1. Cooking, American — Southern style. I. Rushing, Slade. II. Title.
  TX715.2.S68V557 2012
  641.5975 — dc23
                            2012012084

ISBN 978-1-60774-262-3
eISBN 978-1-60774-263-0

Printed in China

Design by Betsy Stromberg
Prop Styling by Angie Mosier

10 9 8 7 6 5 4 3 2 1

First Edition